10.95

CW01636624

BURNING for Freedom

BURNING for Freedom

A Theology of the Black Atlantic Struggle for Liberation

Delroy A. Reid-Salmon

IAN RANDLE PUBLISHERS
Kingston • Miami

First published in Jamaica, 2012 by
Ian Randle Publishers
11 Cunningham Avenue
Box 686
Kingston 6
www.ianrandlepublishers.com

National Library of Jamaica Cataloguing-In-Publication Data

Reid-Salmon, Delroy A.
Burning for Freedom : A Theology of the Black Atlantic Struggle for Liberation / Delroy A. Reid-Salmon

p. ; cm.
Bibliography : p. - Includes index
ISBN 978-976-637-538-6 (pbk)

1. Black theology 2. Liberation theology 3. Sharpe, Sam, d. 1832
4. Racism – Religious aspects 5. Jamaica – History – Slave insurrection, 1831
I. Title

230.08996 - dc 22

Cover and Book Design by Ian Randle Publishers
Printed and Bound in the United States of America

DEDICATION

I dedicate this book to Sam Sharpe and his fellow Freedom Fighters who paid the ultimate price to ensure that liberation became a reality for all but especially for the poor and the oppressed. Such faith is admirable, commitment imitable and courage inspiring.

Table of Contents

Acknowledgements

This project would not have come to fruition without the vision, support and encouragement of many people, too numerous to mention individually. I am grateful to all. I must mention, however, those who have played a role beyond the call of duty.

I am thankful to Ian Randle Publishers for the confidence they have in the project. I deeply appreciate Ian Randle for his admirable professionalism, good advice and breath of vision that inspired me in writing this book. I am particularly grateful to Christine Randle for her patience and understanding that helped to sustain me throughout the long, tedious and demanding journey of writing as well.

My deepest appreciation goes to Wale Hudson-Roberts, who stirred the fire of my interest in Sam Sharpe, Anthony Reddie who helped me to conceptualize and strengthen the idea of this book. Thanks especially to Winsome Williams for proof-reading the manuscript, assisting in preparing the references and displaying great interest in the whole project; Lynnette Mullings for reading and offering helpful critique of the introduction, chapters one, seven and the conclusion; Lerleen Willis for providing remarkable stylistic and substantive suggestions of the entire manuscript; Joseph Anderson for facilitating my field-trip to the site of the former Kensington Estate and Frank Williams for giving technical support and sharing the vision. I am especially grateful to Verene Shepherd who not only read and critiqued the full manuscript but made significant constructive suggestions that helped me to clarify and strengthen my argument. Thanks particularly to Neville Blythe who encouraged me and insisted that this book should be published but never lived to see it become a reality.

Of course, the Oxford Centre for Christianity and Culture, Regent's Park College, has played a pivotal role in my writing this book by providing the forum and the context for doing the research and developing my ideas. Thanks to Paul Fiddes for his visionary and passionate commitment to theological scholarship, Nicholas Wood for his generous hospitality and consistent and strong support and John Briggs for his wise advice, critical insights and practical suggestions.

Thanks also to the librarians at the Jamaica National Library, Angus Library, Regent's Park College and Bodleian Library of Commonwealth and African Studies, Oxford University for their patience, understanding and resourcefulness.

From the inception of writing this book, the church I pastor, Grace Baptist Chapel, has not only supported but embraced the work. For this, I am more than thankful. Above all, the members of the Wednesday Evening Prayer Service continue to be a tower of strength and reliable sojourners. Their soldier-like spirit and deep faith have carried me throughout the writing process. What a gift it is to be the pastor of a church so generous, visionary and wise.

I am grateful to my mother Joyce, for doing only what mothers can do to prepare a son for an arduous undertaking and for the special times we shared discussing the ideas in this book and the work of these Freedom Fighters. Thanks also to my nephew Malique for accompanying me on my field trip to Sam Sharpe Square and the former Kensington Estate, for asking those pertinent and searching questions, expressing deep interest, reminding me of the reasons for this study and for encouraging me that a generation will come to know, better understand and appreciate Sam Sharpe.

Above all, much thanks to my wife Elaine whose interest in the work, generous heart, joyful spirit, great hope for the future and unconditional support cheered me on, especially during the 'desert' stages of this journey.

For everyone and the opportunity to write this book, I give God thanks.

Introduction

This study argues that the Sam Sharpe Revolt was a revelation of the will of God for the liberation of the enslaved and oppressed similar to the biblical story of the Exodus of the Hebrew people from Pharaoh's oppression in Egypt (Exod. 3:7–10). This understanding is expressed by a British Baptist missionary, John May, in a tribute to Sam Sharpe.

The Demon of Thraldom rushed on like a flood,
And the land of its guilt was empurpled with blood,
For long had it rolled in its maddened career,
E'er the corpse, honored Sharpe, was stretched out on its bier.
The Martyr has fallen, but the palm of the Free
Waves proud o'er the British West Indian Sea.

The Spirit of Freedom moves forth o'er the deep,
And the elements wake from the silence of sleep;
True, the strife may be fierce, but the Herald of Light
Speaks of Beauty, and Order, and Quiet, and Right,
Move on, blessed Agent! Till all shall be free,
O'er every nation and every sea.[1]

This noble claim reflects the extent to which some church leaders understood Sharpe's Revolt. It comes, however, with some measure of surprise that given the stubborn resistance to the liberation of the enslaved, a British missionary, a member of the oppressive system and beneficiary of the hegemonic structure had the courage to offer such extraordinary tribute to one like Sam Sharpe. It certainly affirms the view that the Sam Sharpe Revolt was the application of God's will to the social and historical reality. Essentially, the Sam Sharpe Revolt can be understood as a reading and interpreting of the message of the Biblical Witness for the transformation and liberation of human life and society.

In order to facilitate an orderly discussion of this study, it is important to provide a general overview of the structure of the book. This overview includes a description of the genesis of this study on the Sam Sharpe Revolt, the reasons and significance of this scholarly undertaking, definitions of some key terminologies and the contents of this volume.

How The Study Began

Three significant events shaped the context for the development of the central thesis of this book. The first was a conference observing the 200th Anniversary of the Slave Trade Act, held at Regent's Park College, University of Oxford, April 2007. As a collaborative effort between the aforementioned institution and the Baptist Union of Great Britain, Wale Hudson-Roberts, the Racial Justice Director, invited me to present a paper on Sam Sharpe. I offered the paper, 'Faith on Fire,' as an exploratory study on the role of faith in Black liberation struggle. In this paper, it is argued that the faith of the enslaved played a central role in their liberation. Although not much scholarly attention has been given to this concern, my paper was an initial attempt to formulate a theological interpretation of this struggle for liberation.

The second event that contributed to the development of the thesis of this book was another conference also held in observance of the 200th Anniversary of the Slave Trade Act at the Queens Foundation for Ecumenical Theological Education in Birmingham, United Kingdom on 13–15 July 2007. At the invitation of Anthony Reddie, Research Fellow and Consultant in Black Theological Studies for the British Methodist Church at said institution, I presented a paper on Sam Sharpe, 'Faith and the Gallows,' as an opportunity to further develop the work started at the previous conference at Regent's Park College.

The paper argued that having faith in Jesus Christ costs and as such, the execution of Sam Sharpe was an example of the price the oppressed may have to pay for their liberation. Interestingly, this paper is included in a forth coming volume, edited by Anthony Reddie, entitled, *Black Theology, Slavery and Contemporary Christianity,* published by Ashgate Publishing Group.

The third event that contributed to the development of the idea of a theology of the Black Atlantic struggle for liberation and the writing of this book is my appointment as a Research Fellow at the Oxford Centre for Christianity and Culture at Regent's Park College. My work enjoys the enthusiastic support and great encouragement of Paul Fiddes, professor of systematic theology, Director of Research and then Principal of Regent's Park College and Nicholas Wood, Dean of the college and Director of the Oxford Centre for Christianity and Culture.

Through this institution, they provided the context and intellectual space and resources for me to pursue the research on the subject and writing of this book.

A year after my appointment as a fellow, I began working on 'The Sam Sharpe Project' as one my primary research and writing projects. This work has culminated in the observance of the first international conference on Sam Sharpe, on the theme, 'Sam Sharpe and the Quest for Human liberation: History, Theology and Legacy' at the University of Oxford, 13–16 April 2010. This groundbreaking, epoch-making historical event not only attracted leading scholars from Britain, Jamaica and the United States of America, but represented the first academic conference in general and the first theological conference in particular on Sam Sharpe at the University of Oxford.

Historiographical Challenges and Approach

The studying of Sam Sharpe poses a historiographical challenge. In the first instance, Sam Sharpe was literally invisible until after his Revolt and subsequent execution on 23 May 1832. Prior to these events, the authorities did not know of him. Indeed, it is reasonable to assert that what is known about Sharpe is after the fact and that any knowledge of him would be clouded by and even understood through one single event. It is no surprise that the major newspaper, *The Jamaica Watchman,* which reported the views of the other newspapers, has between January[2] and June 1832,[3] only two references to Sharpe. One was the warrant for his arrest and the other, a detailed account of his execution. Thus, his sudden appearance and quick disappearance from the stage of history could suggest that Sharpe's life was clothed in mystery as well as reflect the deft ability of a slave-holding society to silence and erase threats to the status quo.

The mystery surrounding Sam Sharpe's life and the scarcity of information on him make obtaining information about Sharpe very difficult. What we know of him is essentially a work of imagination. While historians may have written interpretive accounts about Sharpe, the most comprehensive and definitive accounts are fictionalized portrayal of his life and work. This includes works such as, Vic Reid's, *Peter of Ephraim,*[10] Fred Kennedy's, *Daddy Sharpe*[11] and the most recent, Andrea Levy's, *The Long Song.*[12] Thus, the veracity of the historicity of Sharpe's life is largely the product of assembling pieces of information and filling in the gaps with informed assumptions and visionary perceptions[13] as is discussed in chapter one.

The second historiographical challenge in undertaking this study on Sam Sharpe is the means through which we know about him. What is known about Sharpe came primarily through and from the perspective of the European colonizers. As such, we have a colonized knowledge and version of Sharpe. In which case, how Sharpe was viewed, defined and described was subjective, negative and partial. For example, the primary sources about Sharpe are all provided by European male, Methodist and Baptist missionaries, Henry Bleby,[4] Thomas Burchell,[5] and William Knibb.[6] To date, there is no other primary source of knowledge about Sharpe except the warrant for his arrest[7] and the Court Records of his trial.[8] Therefore, inherent in our knowledge about Sharpe is a bias towards the dominant society which instinctively, elicit from this scholar, the application of the hermeneutic of suspicion,[9] a method and process of understanding and exposing the ideological biases in intellectual discourses as in this instance, historical interpretation.

Thus, these factors of invisibility, fragmentation and scarcity warrant a leap of faith in order to establish the historicity of persons, like Sharpe. In this regard, the role of theologian is central. The theologian uses the known to connect the past with the present to engender a sense of continuity. With this leap of faith, the theologian engages in the imaginative endeavour of listening carefully to the voice of history, paying close attention to the wisdom of tradition and availing one's self to the oral accounts of the violent memory of the forgotten people of African descent. In this case, the theologian not only facilitates and interprets the experience for the people in light of faith in Jesus Christ but engages in the creative work of theological reconstruction.

Defining Some Key Terms:

A. Black Atlantic

This book is a work of theological construction. It constructs a theology of the Black Atlantic experience. In the most general terms, Black refers to people of African descent. Used in this inclusive sense, Black can be understood as self-designation or the identity of people of African heritage. In a more specific sense, the term refers to the people who are shaped and affected by the experience of suffering and oppression due to slavery, colonialism and racism or white supremacy and are involved in the struggle for liberation from these hegemonic and demonic principalities and powers.

Building on the British thinker, Paul Gilroy's usage of the term 'Black Atlantic' as a framework for constructing 'nationality, location, identity, and historical memory,'[14] the term was employed to encapsulate the theological meaning of the experience of this body of people. Gilroy accentuates the fluidity of this identity and culture. He argues that regardless of their place of resident, people of African descent are always on the move due to voluntary or forced migration. It is this phenomenon of movement not only as a reality of Black existence but as a prophetic critique of the dominant society, the reggae artist Robert N. Marley describes in his classic song, 'Exodus.'

Exodus, all right! Movement of Jah people!
Open your eyes and look within:
Are you satisfied with the life you're living?
We know where we're going;
We know where we're from.
We're leaving Babylon, y'all!
We're going to our Father's land

Jah come to break downpression,
Rule equality,
Wipe away transgression,
Set the captives free.[15]

With the changes that occur in identity and culture due to migration and other factors, it can be argued that faith in God, the Liberator of the oppressed is the single constant factor in the Black Atlantic struggle for liberation. Faith may be expressed in different ways in terms of ideological and theological perspectives but affirmed is the constancy of faith as a resource and the theological dimension of the Black struggle for liberation.

B. A Theology of the Black Atlantic Struggle for Liberation

What do we mean by a theology of the Black Atlantic Struggle for Liberation? Theology is the critical study about God. The concern in this study is not about the being or nature of God but about the meaning of this experience in light of faith in the God revealed in Jesus Christ. The study asks questions such as: what is the meaning of the Black experience? Black people have been fighting for liberation, seeking a better life, what does this struggle mean? What does God have to do with it? Why do Black people have to be struggling the way they do? Put differently, the study asks what are the causes for this struggle, examines the Black experience according to God's revelation in Jesus Christ and considers what actions are to be taken to appropriate God's will especially if the situation is contrary to God's will.

Thus, a theology of the Black Atlantic struggle for liberation is an interpretation of the meaning of God in light of the experience from the perspective of Black people of the Diaspora including but not limited to Britain, the Caribbean and the United States of America. While Black theology in these contexts deals with their particular issues, a theology of the Black Atlantic struggle concerns the common global issues such as religious practices, identity, suffering and oppression, migration, history, memory and hope and other matters related and deriving from our common experience and shared life that is symbolized through the Sam Sharpe Revolt.

Rationale and Significance

Why this book? Why the interest in the Sam Sharpe Revolt? Indeed, the Sam Sharpe Revolt is regarded as the most widespread and greatest of all enslaved peoples' revolts in the so-called British Commonwealth in terms of the number of enslaved involved, the area it covered and what it portended in the aftermath. For example, the Revolt took place in an area of over 700 square miles, involved more than 60,000 enslaved persons and 600 people died by execution and other means carried out by the government.[16] As historian Michael Craton argues; 'By any account the 1831–32 Jamaican uprising – alternatively called the Christmas Rebellion or the Baptist War – served as a momentous climax to the long history of British West Indian slave resistance.'[17]

Thus, the Sam Sharpe Revolt can be considered along with the Haitian Revolution of 1791–1803[18], the greatest manifestations of resistance that led to the abolition of the institution and practice of slavery in the Black Atlantic world.

But in studying the Sam Sharpe Revolt, it is detected that within the Caribbean intellectual tradition, the body of thought that constitutes the historical and theoretical framework for interpreting life through the prism of the Black Atlantic experience[19], has not taken into account the centrality of the Christian Faith in the quest for liberation from oppression and for the fullness of life. This Caribbean tradition of thinking focuses primarily on the political aspects of life oblivious to the theological dimension which events such as the Sam Sharpe Revolt symbolizes. For example, liberation theologians have employed a socio-political or materialist informed analysis in their work. The issue in question, however, is not the materialist ideological perspective, but the absence of critical insight into the importance of revelation and the place of faith and God in the process of liberation.

This study, therefore, reasserts the centrality of the Christian Faith as the centre for the commitment to emancipation. It challenges the notions of the non-confessional and socio-political basis for human liberation. It is argued that these notions of doing theology ignore the role of the Christian Faith and ultimately provide a humanistic materialist, a human-centred interpretation of Black liberation.[20] With this perspective, this book also serves as a polemical riposte to both the non-confessional expression of Black religion and Christianity[21] that are represented in works such as Anthony B. Pinn's *Why Lord: Suffering and Evil in Black Theology,* Noel L. Erskine's *From Garvey to Marley: Rastafari Theology,* and non-liberative interpretation of faith in Joseph D. Aldred's, *Respect: Understanding Caribbean British Theology* and Thabiti M. Anyabwile, *The Decline of African American Theology: From Biblical Faith to Cultural Captivity.*

Moreover, this study offers an alternative view to these notions of liberation. While some would want to dismiss and marginalize religion as if it played no part in the liberation of the enslaved and other oppressed people and that religion has no relevance to the public arena and should be relegated to private life,[22] it should be demonstrated that it was not the slave-holding oppressive version of Christianity that played this role but the liberating religion of the enslaved. Their religion was different from that of the Euro-American Christianity. The enslaved saw the religion of the enslavers as a distortion of the truth and misrepresentation of true religion and God. As biblical prophet Isaiah asked: Is not true religion to 'lose the chains of injustice and untie the cords of the yoke [*oppression*] and to set the oppressed free ...' (Isaiah 58:6ff).

In addition to functioning as an analytical tool in the sense of Paul Gilroy's *Black Atlantic: Modernity and Double Consciousness* and Michelle Ann Stephens *Black Empire: The Masculine Global Imagery of Caribbean Intellectuals in the United States, 1914–1962*, the study further engages the Black Atlantic experience as a source for theological discourse employing the Sam Sharpe Revolt as a paradigm. As this study asserts, the Revolt undermined the social, political, moral and theological foundations of British imperialism as well as Western social and intellectual traditions.

The specificity of Black existence and humanity as a paradigm will be used to construct a theology of the Black Atlantic struggle for liberation. Essentially, this book explores the relationship between faith and human liberation by examining how the Sam Sharpe Revolt can function as an historical event, heuristic framework and source for theological discourse.

The Structure of the Book

The following chapters focus on finding a way to advance the view that the Sam Sharpe Revolt was a manifestation of the will of God for the liberation of the oppressed as an effort to demonstrate that faith can make a difference in the world.

Chapter one provides an introduction to Sam Sharpe. While not a biographical account, the chapter provides the reader with some key insights into this significant figure whose life and work the book utilizes to construct a theology of the Black Atlantic experience. At the same time, it demonstrates that the human experience is a source for theological discourse as human life reveals the relationship between God and humanity.[23]

Chapter two identifies the different perspectives of the Sam Sharpe

Revolt. Taking into account the dominant understandings of the Revolt, the chapter offers an alternative view. This view not only incorporates the others but argues for a theological understanding of the Revolt. As such, the chapter establishes the centrality of faith, theology in Black struggle for and to demonstrate the meaning and relevance of the Sam Sharpe Revolt for contemporary society.

Chapter three looks at the social context in which Sam Sharpe lived by examining the factors that shaped his faith, the encounter between Black religion and Euro-American Christianity and the implications of such encounters for Black theology. With the depravation of liberty and the brutality of plantation society as the major aspects of Sharpe's society, exploring his social context allows theology to delve into existential reality in order to excavate a faith that informs and inspires liberation.

Chapter four offers a descriptive account of the trend to situate Black liberation outside a Christocentric framework. The chapter identifies two components of this trend contending that this is an attempt to advocate an understanding of liberation without faith. Here the notion of a non-confessional and non-liberative Black theology is discussed. As an alternative to this approach, a Christocentric basis and model of Black theology is preferred.

Chapter five discusses the meaning of faith in Jesus and how this might address the relationship between faith and liberation within the context of the Black Atlantic experience. Yet, what are the contents of this faith when it relates to liberation? The chapter uses faith as practised by Sam Sharpe as a paradigm to demonstrate the confessional nature and Christological basis of a theology of the Black Atlantic struggle for liberation

Chapter six focuses on the power of the powerless. With the understanding that the Sam Sharpe Revolt was a theological act, it is necessary to establish the basis of such a bold claim. Central to this claim is the notion of 'the power of the powerless.' Arguing, therefore, that the oppressed are instruments of their own liberation, the chapter delineates the theological framework of the Revolt and simultaneously demonstrates the basis of the power of those who are regarded as powerless.

Chapter seven addresses the relationship among the Black Atlantic

Diasporan people. The lack of a common identity, the broken bond of kinship, persistent oppression and the absence of a united purpose in the context of a globalized world calls for a theological response. Using the Sam Sharpe Revolt as a paradigm for this linkage, the chapter examines the historical, cultural and theological factors that constitute a Black Atlantic, Diasporan identity and kinship.

Chapter eight interprets the theological meaning of the Sam Sharpe Revolt. The view is advanced that faith is essential to Black liberation, the transformation of society and human living. The chapter urges that through the Sam Sharpe Revolt, God was reordering the structures of society and will continue to do so today. This could be seen to demonstrate that faith in Jesus Christ is not an abstract idea in the mind but a truth to be lived.

Ultimately, the book pays particular attention to the socio-religious context of faith, the historicization of faith, the connection of the Black Diasporan, and the theological implications and legacy of the Revolt and some of the challenges of emancipatory praxis. Certainly, *Burning for Freedom* articulates a distinct Christian theology of the Black struggle for liberation. With this intent, this book heeds the command of God: 'Speak up for those who cannot speak for themselves, for the rights of all who are destitute. Speak up and judge fairly; defend the rights of the poor and needy' (Prov. 31:8–9; NIV). It is to this task, we now turn.

Notes

1. E. Wolley, 'The Land of the Free,' (Cincinnati: Caleb Clark, 1847), 15.
2. The *Jamaica Watchman*, 4 January 1832.
3. The *Jamaica Watchman*, 2 June 1832.
4. Henry Bleby, *The Death Struggles of Slavery*, (London: Hamilton, Adams and Co., 1853); 113–20. See also, C. S. Reid, *Samuel Sharpe: From Slave To National Hero* (Kingston: The Bustamante Institute of Public and International Affairs, 1988), 54–59; 88–95.
5. William F. Burchell, *Memoir of Thomas Burchell: Twenty-Two Year a Missionary in Jamaica* (London: Benjamin L. Green, *1849*), 100–81.
6. John Howard Hinton, *Memoir of William Knibb, Missionary in Jamaica 1849)* (Bristol: Houlston and Stoneman, 1849), 111–40.
7. Cited in C. S. Reid, *Samuel Sharpe: From Slave To National Hero* (Kingston: The Bustamante Institute of Public and International Affairs, 1988), 54.
8. Cited in Reid, 89–94.

9. See for example, Jose Miguez-Binino, 'Marist Critical Tools: Are They Helpful in breaking the Stronghold of Idealist hermeneutics,' in *Voices from the Margins: Interpreting the Bible in Third World,* ed. R. S. Sugirtharajah (New York: Orbis Books, 1995), 58–68.
10. V. S. Reid, *Peter of Ephraim* (Kingston: Jamaica Publishing House, 1971).
11. Fred Kennedy, *Daddy Sharpe: A Narrative of the Life and Adventures of Samuel Sharpe, A West Indian Slave Written by Himself, 1832* (Kingston: Ian Randle Publishers, 2008).
12. Andrea Levy, *The Long Song* (New York: Farrar, Straus and Giroux, 2010).
13. Edward K. Brathwaite, *Wars of Respect: Nanny and Sharpe* (Kingston: Agency For Public Information, 1977), 7.
14. Paul Gilroy, *The Black Atlantic: Modernity and Double Consciousness* (New York: Verso, 1993), 16.
15. Robert Nesta Marley, 'Exodus' (Kingston: Island Records Ltd, 1977).
16. Mary Turner, *Slaves and Missionaries: The Disintegration of Jamaican Slave Society, 1787–1834* (Kingston: The Press University of the West Indies, 1998), 161. See also, Edward Kamau Braithwaite, 'The Slave Rebellion in the Great River Valley of St James –1831/32,' *Jamaica Historical Review,* Vol. XII (1982): 11–31.
17. Michael Craton, *Testing the Chains* (Ithaca: Cornel University Press, 1982), 293.
18. C. L. R. James, *The Black Jacobs: Toussaint L'Ouverture and the San Domingo Revolution* (New York: Vintage Book, 1983).
19. Gordon K. Lewis, *Main Currents in Caribbean Thought: The Historical Evolution of Caribbean Society in its ideological Aspects, 1492–1999* (Baltimore: John Hopkins University Press, 1983); Bill Schwarz, ed., *West Indian Intellectuals in Britain* (Manchester: Manchester University Press, 2003); Denis Benn, *The Caribbean; An Intellectual History, 1774–2003* (Kingston: Ian Randle Publishers, 2004); Silvio Torres-Saillant, *An Intellectual History of the Caribbean* (New York: Palgrave Macmillan, 2006).
20. Frederick L. Ware, *Methodologies of Black Theology* (Ohio: The Pilgrim Press, 2002), 114.
21. For a study on the Modalities of Black theology in the American context, see Fredrick L. Ware, *Methodologies of Black Theology* (Cleveland: The Pilgrim Press, 2002); Regarding the British context, see Anthony G. Reddie, *Working Against the Grain: Re-imaging Black Theology in the 21st Century* (London: Equinox Publishing Ltd., 2008), 9–34. To date, there is no study on the modalities of Caribbean theology but I am working

on a forthcoming volume.

22. Robert C. Tucker, ed., *The Marx-Engels Reader*, 2nd Ed., (New York: Norton, 1978), 28–25.
23. James Wm. McClendon, Jr., *Biography as Theology* (Philadelphia: Trinity Internal Press, 1990), 67–88.

1 - Sam Sharpe:
The Man Behind the 'Legend'

INTRODUCTION

Sam Sharpe is one of the most significant and successful leaders in the Black Atlantic experience and history. He was a deacon in the orthodox Baptist church and leader in the Black community who led the 'Great Jamaican Enslaved Revolt' of 1831.[1] Providing an adequate theological interpretation of this radical historical event requires having, at least, some basic knowledge about this distinctive person.

Knowing about Sam Sharpe, however, is a challenge as was already noted in the introductory chapter. Without rehearsing what was discussed, it is a challenge because we know very little about him. What we know about him are what scholars have gleaned from news reports, government documents and church records to construct a biography of this venerable man. The information, therefore, about his life is not only scant but fragmentary and inconsistent as historian Edward Braithwaite observes:

> *Indeed, there is every indication that neither missionaries nor Government officials knew whether they were dealing with Sam or John Throp or Tharp or Sharp; and whether they were dealing with a slave from Croydon, Hazelymph Catadupa or Cooper's Hill and whether his owner was a male solicitor or female then residing at Montego Bay, or a man called Gray.[2]*

Braithwaite's observation underscores one of the difficulties scholars face in studying the life and work of enslaved persons. For example, Sam Sharpe, as an enslaved person, did not feature in the historical records significantly except as a result of revolutionary actions. Baptist pastor-scholar, Clarence Reid expresses this view as follows:

> *If Sam Sharpe had not raised a revolt, his name like that of countless other slaves, would have disappeared completely. For no-one was interested in the biographical details of a slave. He was a non-person, a chattel. The pedigree of a horse is better documented today than that of a slave.[3]*

Attesting to this claim, Reid emphasizes that not even in his native country, Jamaica, where he was made a national hero in 1975, was Sam Sharpe well known.[4] The issue in question, however, is not about Sam Sharpe the person but his work. Reid notes:

> *...To the extent to which the 'Baptist War' initiated by Sam Sharpe, affected the flow of the struggle that led to the Abolition of the Slave System in the British Empire, to that extent it may be claimed that our National Hero in his bid for freedom, has earned a niche in the social History of the World of the Nineteenth Century.*[5]

Notwithstanding this claim and the paucity of information about Sam Sharpe, this chapter is an attempt to provide a descriptive portrayal of Sam Sharpe. This portrayal is intended to provide vital resources in helping us to grasp the significance and construction of a theology of the Black Atlantic struggle for liberation. In light of this purpose, the discussion attends primarily to the personal, social and intellectual and moral factors that describe the identity of Sam Sharpe.

Personal Identity

Sam Sharpe lived a relatively brief life. Sharpe was born in St James, Jamaica. We do not know the precise date of his birth but it is believed that he was born 1800.[6] What we certainly know is that he was executed by the British government on 23 May 1832.[7] He lived, then, for 31 years.[8] He was given the name of his enslaver, Samuel Sharpe, a lawyer and the proprietor of the Coopers Hill Estate in Montego Bay, St James.[9] Sam Sharpe, the enslaved, however, was also known within the Black and enslaved community of his time as 'Daddy Sharpe,' 'Ruler Sharpe' and 'preacher to the rebels'[10] because he was one of, if not their primary leader.[11]

Another element of Sharpe's personal identity is his physical features. The British Methodist clergyman, Henry Bleby, who personally knew Sharpe and was an eyewitness to his execution, describes Sharpe in his resourceful book, *Death Struggles of Slavery*. He describes Sharpe as a person with an indomitable presence. Bleby states:

> *He was of middle size, his fine sinewy frame was handsomely*

> *moulded, and his skin as perfect as can be well imagined. His forehead was high and broad while his nose and his lips exhibited the usual characteristics of the Negro race. He had teeth whose regularity and pearly whiteness a court beauty might have envied, and an eye whose brilliancy was almost dazzling.*[12]

Judging from these remarks, Sharpe was undoubtedly a person of African descent. While this is important to know, the intent is not necessarily to identify his ethnicity but to demonstrate how his physical features expressed the role he played in his society.

Vocation

Knowing the personal identity of Sam Sharpe is not enough to tell who he was. We can know more about him through his vocation. He was categorized as a 'domestic slave.' This was a person who worked to maintain the house and attended to the needs and wishes of his or her enslavers. In this regard, Sharpe was more privileged than his fellow enslaved comrades who worked in the field. He not only worked shorter hours, less physically demanding work, but he was better clothed and fed. Mary Turner puts this way of life in perspective. She writes:

> *...when sickly, children from slave village were sent to live at the great house for a few weeks.*[13] *Within a brief period of living in better social conditions, the children's health was restored.' As B. M. Senior notes: 'They very soon evince in their countenances the change in their mode of living, they became fat, sleek, shining...'*[14]

The so-called 'domestic slave' also had more and easier access to the enslaver which in many cases provided the opportunity to become educated or at least, to be able to learn to read and write[15] which was neither normative nor legal. Writing in this regard, Winston Lawson makes the notable remark:

> *What is notable throughout is that the fear that education, both religious and secular might unsettle their* ***enslaved****, minds to the point of turning on them their oppressors, was exceeded only by their perennial paranoia about another Haiti being*

created, if political or military power were taken hold of by the despised under class.[16] [emphasis mine]

Lawson is pointing out the opposition of the ruling class to educate the enslaved. It is unlikely that Sam Sharpe was aware of this particular understanding of education. Fred Kennedy, however, in his profoundly insightful work, *Daddy Sharpe*, surmises how Sharpe may have learned about British society and culture.[17] Kennedy reports in the following imaginary conversation between Sharpe and his so-called owner:

You will become my house servant, Sam and well deserved is this...My mother always had a fondness for you and you very proudly bear my father's name. I shall give you the opportunity to learn to read and write, and in my house you will grow to be a Christian man. But you must always do as I say and always be an obedient servant.[18]

If this were the case, he must have been exposed to the ideas that were intended to domesticate him and make him into an enslaved 'European.' Yet, deducing from these remarks in light of Sharpe's Revolt, he was living in the social and political system but he was not of it. Oral Thomas, in his insightful study on Caribbean biblical interpretation, makes this very powerful observation:

Despite the fact or more precisely because of the fact that Sharpe was treated well and kindly as a domestic slave, Sharpe's location within the social system as a slave located him in a different place socially and ideologically from his owner.[19]

Thomas's argument suggests that Sharpe's vocation reflects the social and ideological systemic distinctions in the society. Sharpe's status has certainly put him at odds with the dominant society. Writing of this situation, Edward Braithwaite notes:

Kind people treat their dogs, cats and horses kindly; but kind treatment for slaves is like putting expensive and beautiful clothes on the back of a leper. The beautiful clothes do not change the condition of the leper. Kind treatment does not change the condition of a slave...Slavery is the greatest violation of the human spirit; kindness does not correct the violation. Only freedom can.[20]

Braithwaite is correct when he argues that the vocation of a 'domestic slave' does not change one's status from an enslaved to a freedom person. In order to be a free person, it is to know that individual privileges without social transformation are fragile and relative. In fact, individualized freedom attests to the notion that oppression is not only personal but systemic. This is precisely what Sharpe's Revolt indicates. Thomas puts it succinctly: 'For Sharpe, it was not so much he or any other individual was treated but how the whole socio-economic and political machinery was built to dominate and exploit blacks and grant social privilege and rank to whites.'[21]

Clearly, Sharpe did not allow his vocation as a 'domesticate slave' to define his mission in life or undermine his commitment to liberation and solidarity with the oppressed but he used his vocation as counterforce to subvert the unjust social order. Indeed, Sharpe's use of his vocation suggests that he understood that oppression is structural and as such, it demands structural changes. Thus, reflecting the prophet character of Moses as the Bible writer reported (Heb. 11:24–26) and as dramatized by Philip Sherlock in his *Shout for Freedom*,[22] Sharpe employed his vocation as a counter-cultural prophetic force.

Brilliant Mind

Sam Sharpe's personal identity and vocation are not the only factors that tell us who he was. His brilliant mind is also one of his definitive characteristics. We learn about Sharpe's intellectual ability from the British Methodist missionary, Henry Bleby. Sharpe was in jail for leading the Revolt against slavery. Bleby visited him and during his visits, he learned this truth about Sharpe's mighty intellect. Bleby's writes: 'I had an opportunity of observing that he possessed intellectual and oratorical powers above the common order and this was the secret of the extensive influence which he exercised.'[23] Bleby goes into greater detail to describe Sharpe's enormous intellectual capacity and ability.

> *I heard him two or three times deliver a brief extemporaneous address to his fellow prisoners on religious topics...and I was amazed at the power and freedom with which he spoke and at the effect which was produced upon his auditory. He appeared to have the feelings and passions of his hearers completely at*

> *his command and when I listened to him at once, I ceased to be surprised at what Gardner had told me, that when Sharpe spoke to him and others on the subject of slavery, he Gardner was wrought up almost to a state of madness.*[24]

It is arguable that the ability to inspire and persuade others to pursue action they would not have done under normal circumstances attests to the nature of Sharpe's intellect. This perspective underscores the role of the intellect in Black liberation. My understanding of the intellect, however, is certainly not about smartness and cleverness but the mind rooted in the quest for justice, employing ideas, words, language and the totality of one's being as tools to transform society. In effect, as Sharpe has demonstrated, the intellect is indispensable for liberation and transformation of persons and society. Indeed, through his Revolt, Sharpe has modelled the relationship between the life of the mind and human liberation with such moral conviction and political power and spiritual integrity.

The brilliant nature of Sharpe's mind is even more evident in his administrative skills. Sharpe is acknowledged and credited to have been the primary organizer and leader of the Revolt against the system of slavery. From this point of view, Henry Bleby writes:

> *Sam Sharpe was the man whose active brain devised the project, and he had sufficient authority with those around him to carry it into effect, having acquired an extraordinary degree of influence among his fellow slaves.*[25]

Yet, crediting Sharpe for the leadership of the Revolt is not my primary concern. The issue is the organizing of the Revolt which attests to his administrative ability.

The Sam Sharpe Revolt did not take place suddenly or spontaneously but after careful planning, rigorous deliberation and deep thought.[26] Over a period of time, Sharpe has been reading through newspapers that the king of England has abolished slavery.[27] Reporting this understanding to Henry Bleby, Edward Hylton, one of Sharpe's colleagues, stated what Sharpe told them.

> *The king had made the free, or was resolved upon doing it, the white and Grignon were holding secret meetings with doors*

shut close...and had determined to kill all black men, and save all women and children and keep them in slavery.[28]

Inasmuch as Sharpe had every reason to predicate freedom on the law of the country, he based it a mistaken belief. The king of England did not make any law to abolish slavery. Bleby provides clarification of this matter. He states:

This news [about freedom] so imperfectly conveyed, and misunderstood, indelibly stamped upon their minds that the 'free paper' had come and the planters would not give it up. They therefore determined to claim their freedom. To effect this, they held secret meetings, bound themselves by a solemn oath, not to divulge their plans. They resolved that after Xmas holidays in 1831, which usually last one week, they would 'sit down,' that is cease from work until the planters gave up the 'free papers' and paid them wages.[29]

Convinced that their liberation was not becoming a reality, he planned to take it through resistance. He called and conducted a meeting with his companions in the suffering of oppression and the struggle for liberation and informed them about what he read and learned in the newspapers and from discussions among the slaveholders. The testimony of Edward Hylton, one of the leaders of the Revolt, attests to Sharpe's administrative ability through the organization of the Revolt. Hylton described the place and nature of the meeting as well as the number of people who attended. Hylton testified that:

It was during the year 1831, he received a message at Mountain Spring from Sharpe, to meet on the following Saturday at the house of Johnson, at Retrieve estate in St James... At the time appointed, Hylton went to Retrieve, where he met with Sharpe, Johnson and others whom he named. After he held a prayer-meeting, most of the people went away, Sharpe, Johnson and Hylton and few more remaining behind: and the party was afterwards enlarged by several others...'[30]

The leaders and followers were aware of the seriousness of the undertaking and severity of the consequences if they did not succeed. Bleby's report of Edward Hylton's testimony gives penetrating insight into this dimension of the Revolt. Bleby states:

> *Hylton, however, felt that it was a momentous undertaking to which Sharpe was persuading them, and highly dangerous; and that they ought to enter it without the greatest caution. They discussed the matter during the late hours of the night.*[31]

Although they knew that Sharpe was speaking the truth about their freedom, which they too heard and read in the newspapers, Sharpe still had to convince them by taking an oath of kissing the Bible. After they reached agreement on the matter, 'and the plan of operation were fully detailed by Sharpe, the whole party bound themselves together by oath not to work after Christmas as slaves but to assert their claim to freedom, and to be faithful to each other.'[32]

Here we recognize Sharpe's administrative genius in full operation. He required all those who wish to participate in this liberation struggle to commit themselves to abide by these three standards: (1) commitment to the cause of liberation, (2) confidentiality and (3) cooperation/solidarity to each other. In order to prove the sincerity and seriousness of the commitment to the cause, it was sealed by an oath of 'kissing the Bible.' This act of commitment was important not only because the cause was a matter of life and death but also to ensure that the plan would not be revealed to the authorities or told to any one who does not believe in it.

Sharpe's act suggests further that he might have been aware of the failure of other revolts due to betrayal such as that of Gabriel Prosser, Denmark Vesey and Nat Turner in the Unites States.[33] Although it is not being suggested that Sharpe was aware of these failed revolts, his actions reflect an awareness of such possibility. Or, at least, Sharpe knew his Jamaican history of revolts from the 1660s with the arrival of the first group of Africans to the second Maroon War of 1795[34] which we will discuss in chapter three. Sharpe, therefore, was taking the necessary measures to ensure the success of his Revolt.

Fully aware of such possibility, Sharpe was not dissuaded from conducting a series of similar meetings which he operated like a political campaign. He met with other Freedom Fighters and sent his representatives throughout the country to inform and acquire supporters for his plan. For example, in a separate meeting, Sharpe met with some supporters including two of his associates, Gardner and Dove where he spoke to them about the evil of slavery and what he read in the newspapers.[35] In his report to Bleby, Gardner also said that 'Sharpe sent a man named, Edward Ramsey, round to tell all the properties, to tell the people that the free paper had come.'[36]

This mode of communication and publicity gives fuller and clearer understanding of Sharpe's administrative ingenuity. This concurs with the notion that Sharpe had a network of churches[37] that provided numerical support and functioned as the medium of communication for the planned revolt.[38] If this were the case, one could conclude that Sharpe had a social, political and religious movement that resonates with Albert Raboteau's notion of 'The Invisible Institution'[39] and predates the various civil and religious movements throughout the Black Diaspora.[40]

The Sam Sharpe Revolt took place in Western Jamaica but given the scope of the Revolt, Sharpe and his associates must have travelled extensively, an area of over 600 miles, to the various estates primarily in the parishes of Trelawny, St James, Hanover, Westmoreland and St Elizabeth.[41] The impact of the Revolt, nevertheless, was felt in the Northern parishes of St Ann and St Mary as well as in the central parish of Manchester.[42] Historian, Barry Higman, concurring with my claim of Sharpe's astute mind, declares: 'The rebellion of 1831/32 showed clear evidence of detailed planning, beginning months before the outbreaks, making use of the networks of communication provided by secret trails, the internal market system and the circuit churches.'[43]

The commonly held view of this event is that Sharpe never intended for it to result into a Revolt.[44] It was a 'work stoppage' or industrial action he organized in order to obtain better wages for the enslaved labourers and their liberation from the bondage of slavery.[45] In the event, however, that the slaveholders and the military were to use violence against them, they were to defend themselves. As Bleby reports:

> *'Sharpe's plan was "passive resistance" and they were only to use violence only in case the "buckras" used force to compel them to turn out to work as slaves.'*[46]

While the testimony of Sharpe indicates that the event was a non-violent resistance, his actions suggest otherwise. It was certainly not a plan of genocide, to kill white people as some argue,[47] but it was more than passive resistance. Given the extensive detailed planning, extensive organization and the scope of the problem, the Sam Sharpe Revolt did not suggest a non-violent act. It was a Revolt against a wicked and evil system that dehumanized human beings and denied them their God given freedom. Sharpe stated this very clearly when he said that 'he did not wish to destroy the estates, nor did he desire that any person should be injured; his only object was to obtain freedom.'[48]

Pertaining to the organization of the Revolt, it was a four-phased liberation event with date, time, place and course of action[49] decided. The date scheduled was 27 December 1831 to begin at Kensington Estate in the parish of St James. As an indication that the event was set in motion, a trash house was lit with fire. The trash house at the Palmyra Estate also in St James was also set on fire when those who lived there saw the fire. The other estates leaders and people on neighbouring estates did likewise. The Scottish Presbyterian missionary, Hope Waddell, writing of this event states:

> *It was not long past my usual time when I got back to Cornwall, and there I found confusion and dismay. The congregation which had assembled was dispersing in affright, and would not return to my call. The only answer or explanation that could be got was – 'Palmyra on fire.' It was not an ordinary estate fire they spoke of, which neighboring estate's people would haste to put out. Were it even so, it need have caused us no alarm, there being range of wooded hills between it and Cornwall. It was the pre-concerted signal for our part of the country that the struggle for freedom had begun.*[50]

Waddell's remarks suggest that the enormity and execution of the fire reflects the calibre of the leadership of the Revolt. The leadership not only timed but designed the act as part of an organized plan. Gaining insights from Bleby's account of Sharpe's life, Winston Lawson in his very resourceful book, *Religion and Race: African and European Roots in Conflict – a Jamaican Testament* underscores the notion of Sharpe as a visionary religious leader by crediting him with providing the philosophical and theological framework for it. Lawson states:

> *Sharpe and his colleagues bravely led the revolt against the*

> *socio-economic and political control of the island's resources by the plantocracy and paid the ultimate price for their bold venture in self-determination.*[51]

Before coming to this conclusion, Lawson examines the social context of Sam Sharpe. He explains that the society was undergoing social, economic, political and religious crisis. This ranged from natural disasters to religious conflicts. Sharpe was aware of these problems and with the support of his colleagues, developed their liberation plan.[52] Lawson's observation gives an important insight into this assertion when he argues that Sharpe ventured into an explosive political and religious environment due primarily to economic hardship, the extent of which, the county's leadership did know.[53] This leads Lawson to conclude that Sam Sharpe was:

> *The product of an out-moded agricultural system in which mis-management of the plantations and a complete absence of any vision of what possibilities existed for new technologies and experimental agriculture, at a time of growing competition on the world market, was the norm.*[54]

Model Leader

Most important to our discussion is the understanding of Sharpe and his comrades as exemplary or model leaders. They embodied their belief in freedom as is discussed in chapter eight. But for now, living the Christian Faith is worth mentioning, which Bleby clearly acknowledged Sharpe to have demonstrated: According to Bleby, Sharpe felt 'acutely the degradation and the monstrous injustice of the system and was bent upon its overthrow.'[55] Sharpe was fuelled with passion to destroy the slave system as noted in his bodily expressions and transformation whenever he had the opportunity to speak to the issue. Bleby's description is vivid; '[*Sharpe*] his frame expanded and his eagle-eye seemed to shoot forth rays of light...'[56]

Winston Lawson concurs with this observation with this insightful statement: 'They went to the gallows with evident pride in their conscientious efforts in the cause of freedom and justice outside the parameters, or even within the traditional plantation society.'[57] The

Presbyterian missionary, Hope Waddell, in his eyewitness account of the execution of these Freedom Fighters affirms this claim in describing the dignity and joy with which they faced death:

> *They were all, on the day previous to their execution, put into two large carts, drawn by oxen, each prisoner pinioned, with rope on his neck and a white cap on his head. In this dress they were seated side by side in the carts, and, on moving off from the jail door, they simultaneously commenced hymn, in which all joined with great composure and fervency...and the voice of praise was heard at a distance, ascending from the midst of the mournful cavalcade....On each of the melancholy occasions, the unfortunate men met their death, with a fortitude and cool deliberation that astonished all who beheld them.* [58]

Waddell continues to describe the impact such courage had on his own life. He writes: 'And one cannot but lament the fate, as well as the crimes, of heroic men, who staked all on one great throw for freedom, lost it, and submitted to the dreadful consequences with dignity.'[59]

The courageous dignity of these Freedom Fighters is not limited to one eyewitness. Waddell's Methodist colleague, Henry Bleby had a similar experience in witnessing the execution of Sam Sharpe. He seemed not only to acknowledge the evil of slavery but admired the infectious courage and firm conviction of Sharpe when he said:

> *I could not help feeling deep sorrow and indignation – as I turned from his death scene, and brushed away the tears which the contemplation of his tragical fate called forth – that such as Samuel Sharpe, who possessed a mind...capable of noble things, should be thus immolated at the political shrine of slavery.*[60]

Expressing his thoughts about Sharpe, Bleby attests to the character of the man. Bleby found strength to mourn Sharpe's death and acknowledged – though he may disagree with his chosen means for obtaining freedom – the justice of his cause.

Conclusion

The above confessional statement is not the last word on Sam Sharpe but it helps to tells us who he was. As a person, he exemplifies what it means to be a human being. As servant of the people, he represents a model of prophetic witness. As a leader, he embodies what he is called to do. Yet, this unique person and the significant role he played in society, still does not answer fully the question: Who was Sam Sharpe?

Still, what we have learned so far about Sharpe in terms of his personal identity, vocation and leadership abilities are not adequate to construct a theology of the Black Atlantic struggle for liberation. Building on this foundation, it is necessary to have an understanding of the Revolt. In fact, the identity of Sharpe cannot be properly understood without knowing about the Revolt. How this Revolt is interpreted and understood is discussed in the next chapter.

Notes

1. Edward Braithwaite, 'The Slave Rebellion in the Great River Valley of St James – 1831–32', *Jamaica Historical Review*, Vol. XII (1982): 1–30.
2. Edward Braithwaite, *Wars of Respect: Nanny and Sam Sharpe and the Struggle for People's Liberation* (Kingston: Agency for Public Information, 1977), 23.
3. C. S. Reid, *Samuel Sharpe, From Slave to National Hero* (Kingston: Bustamante Institute of Public and International Affairs, 1988), 56.
4. Reid, 4.
5. Ibid.
6. Edward K. Braithwaite, cited in C.S. Reid's *Samuel Sharpe: From Slave to National Hero*, 59.
7. Henry Bleby, *Death Struggles of Slavery* (London: Hamilton, Adams & Co., 1853), 129.
8. Braithwaite, 28. This date of Sharpe's birth is not a certainty. It could have been at an earlier or later time. More importantly, Braithwaite points out that he was what he termed a creolized African and thus not one who was brought to Jamaica as a slave.
9. Reid, 54–55. Although the identity of Sam Sharpe is uncertain, Reid's perspective represents the general understanding regarding his owner.
10. Reid, 64. Sharpe was also a leader in the orthodox or English Baptist church where the British missionary, Thomas Burchell was pastor. In recognition of Sharpe's prominence in the church and influence among the Black community. Burchell appointed Sharpe to the leadership of the church during his absence to Britain to obtain medical attention due to illness. See for example, Henry Bleby, *Death Struggle*, 116; Mary

Turner, *Slaves and Missionaries*, (Kingston: University of the West Indies Press, 1998), 155.

11. Fred Kennedy, *Daddy Sharpe: A Narrative of the Life and Adventure of Samuel Sharpe, A West Indian Slave Written by Himself, 1832* (Kingston: Ian Randle Publishers, 2008), 28.
12. Henry Bleby, quoted in Reid, 56.
13. Mary Turner, *Slaves and Missionaries: The Disintegration of Jamaican Slave Society, 1787–1834* (Kingston: University of the West Indies Press, 1998), 42.
14. B. M. Senior, *Jamaica as it was, as it is, and as it may be* (London: T. Hurst, 1835), 29.
15. Kennedy, 28–29.
16. Winston Lawson, *Religion And Race: African and European Roots in Conflict - A Jamaican Testament* (New York: Peter Lang Publishing, 1996), 173.
17. Kennedy, 115.
18. Kennedy, 28.
19. Oral Thomas, *Contextual Contestations in Biblical Hermeneutics within a Caribbean Context: A Case for a Biblical Resistant Hermeneutic* (Ph. D. Thesis, University of Birmingham, 2007), 46.
20. Edward K. Braithwaite, 'Sam Sharpe' (Kingston: Jamaica Broadcasting Corporation, 1973).
21. Thomas, 46.
22. Philip Sherlock, *Shout for Freedom; A Tribute to Sam Sharpe* (London: Macmillan Education Ltd, 1976).
23. Henry Bleby, cited in Reid, 56.
24. Henry Bleby cited in Philip Sherlock & Hazel Bennett, *The Story of the Jamaican People* (Kingston: Ian Randle Publishers, 1998), 213.
25. Bleby, 115.
26. Bleby, 110–115.
27. E. Woolley, 'The Land of the Free or A Brief View of Emancipation in the West Indies' (Cincinnati: Caleb Clark, 1947).
28. Bleby, 112.
29. Woolley, 12; see also Henry Bleby 5–6.
30. Bleby, 111.
31. Bleby, 112.
32. Ibid.
33. Gayraud Wilmore, *Black Religion and Black Radicalism: An Interpretation of the Religious History of Afro-American People*, 2nd. Edition (New York: Orbis Press, 1995), 53–73.

34. Philip Sherlock & Hazel Bennett, *The Story of the Jamaican People* (Kingston: Ian Randle Publishers, 1998), 133–49; See also. Michael Craton, *Testing the Chains* (Ithaca: Cornel University Press, 1982), 293–95.
35. Bleby, 114.
36. Ibid.
37. B. W. Higman, *Montpelier Jamaica: A Plantation Community in Slavery and Freedom 1739-1912* (Kingston: University of the West Indies Press, 1998), 262–64; See also, Jean Besson, *Martha Brae's Two Histories: European Expansion and Caribbean Culture – Building in Jamaica* (Chapel Hill: University of North Carolina Press, 2002; Kingston: Ian Randle Publishers, 2003).
38. Mary Turner, *Slaves and Missionaries: The Disintegration of Jamaican Slave Society, 1887-1834* (Kingston: University of the West Indies Press, 1998), 152–53.
39. Albert J. Raboteau, *Slave Religion: The 'Invisible Institution' in the Antebellum South* (New York: Oxford University Press, 1978); See also, Henry H. Mitchell, *Black Church Beginnings: The Long: Hidden Realities of the Firsts Years* (Michigan: Wm. B. Eerdmans Publishing Co., 2004).
40. Rupert Lewis, *Marcus Garvey,* (New Jersey: Africa World Press, Inc., 1988); see also Aldon D. Morris, *The Origins of the Civil Rights Movement: Black Communities Organizing for Change,* (New York: The Free Press, 1984); Taylor Branch, *Parting The Waters: America in the King Years 1954–63* (New York: Touchstone, 1988); Mark Sturge, *Look What The Lord Has Done: An Exploration of Black Christian Faith in Britain* (Bletchley: Scripture Union, 2005).
41. Edward Braithwaite, 'The Slave Rebellion in the Great River Valley of St James –1831–32,' *Jamaica Historical Review,* Vol. XII (1982), 11–31.
42. Turner, 152–69; See also Bleby, 107.
43. Higman, 262–63.
44. Bleby, 116–17.
45. Bleby, 113.
46. Ibid.
47. William Knibb and Peter Borthwick, Colonial Slavery: *Defence of the Baptist Missionaries from the Charge of Inciting the Late Rebellion in Jamaica* (London: The Tourist Office,1832), 3. See also *Twenty-Nine Years in the West Indies and Central Africa* (London: T. Nelson and Co., 1863), 50–59.
48. Bleby, 116–17.
49. These four phases of the Liberation War reflects Sharpe's administrative acumen. There is also the perspective of the Sam Sharpe Revolt

being a 'four-phased' military campaign. It is important to mention this distinction between administrative skills and the nature of the War. My concern is not the structure of this War of Liberation but the administrative abilities of Sharpe. For further discussion on this issue, see for example, Edward Braitwaite, 'Slave Rebellion in the Great River Valley of St James – 1831–32,' *Jamaica Historical Review,* Vol.XII (1982): 11–31.

50. Hope Waddell, *Twenty-Nine Years in the West Indies and Central Africa* (London: T. Nelson and Co., 1863), 53.
51. Winston A. Lawson, *Religion and Race: African and European Roots in Conflict - A Jamaican Testament* (New York: Peter Lang Publishing, 1996), 171.
52. Lawson, 167–68.
53. Lawson, 168.
54. Ibid.
55. Bleby, 118.
56. Bleby, 116.
57. Lawson, 171
58. Hope Waddell, 65.
59. Waddell, 65–67.
60. Bleby, 118.

2 - All Right: Perspectives of the Sam Sharpe Revolt

INTRODUCTION

The struggle for liberation requires that we draw on all the available resources as means of wisdom and empowerment. In this regard, the Sam Sharpe Revolt as a subject of academic study can be a resource for empowerment in fighting structural oppression and effecting transformation in society. This chapter, therefore, concerns how we understand the Sam Sharpe Revolt. Certainly, there are a variety of interpretations of this Revolt such as passive resistance,[1] political act,[2] rebellion[3] or a religious war of liberation.[4]

Given the symbolic and historic significance of the Sam Sharpe Revolt, it should not be surprising that attention is called to the variety of interpretations of this event. While acknowledging that there is no single view of the Revolt, the variety of perspectives demonstrates the scope, the inclusive and holistic character of this event. Regarding the scope of the Revolt, it was not limited to one place, as this study acknowledges, but extended and impacted the trans-Atlantic world in terms of the abolition of slavery and its continued influence on society.

As to the inclusive nature of the Revolt, the variety of perspectives take into account the fact that the Revolt relates and affects every area of life: the social, political, religious and spiritual. These perspectives are not definitive interpretations of the Revolt. Instead, they are representative interpretations of the Revolt from a particular area of learning whether history, politics, religion or any other field.

Essentially, the scope and the inclusive character of the Revolt attest to its holistic character. The variety of perspectives does not compartmentalize, dichotomize or separate life into secular and scared. Rather, the perspectives reflect the understanding and affirmation of life as one reality composed of all the aspects and dimensions of human existence. Thus, the different perspectives of the Sam Sharpe Revolt are expressions of the contextual particularity of the event.

There are two major perspectives to the Sam Sharpe Revolt, the political and the religious. However, in the discussion that follows, these two perspectives are delineated and a third proposed, the theological understanding of the Sam Sharpe Revolt attending to the liberative dimensions. Proposing that the theological perspective best enables us to understand this important and complex event, a variety of social and intellectual sources were used to construct a theology of the Black Atlantic struggle for liberation.

The Political Perspective

The political perspective of the Sam Sharpe Revolt emphasizes social and political transformation of society through the action of the masses. Here the central concern is not the exercise of power but the assertion of human rights[5] and an endeavour to create a more just and equitable society. A cursory review of some of the political understandings of the Revolt reveals two interpretative possibilities, social transformation and industrial action.

Social Transformation

One aspect of the political interpretation is social transformation. Mary Reckford, rejecting the religious view, (to be discussed later in this chapter), argues powerfully in her seminal article, 'The Jamaica Slave Rebellion of 1831,' for the political interpretation of the Sam Sharpe Revolt. She delineates the political context of the Revolt calling attention to the influence the abolitionist movement exerted on the enslaved. She argues that the enslaved were aware of the debate pertaining to the abolition of slavery but the local plantation owners denied them their freedom. Reckford further argues that the enslaved expressed their political discontent through religious means. In making this argument, she states:

> *In the Jamaica protest movement the most important leader, Sam Sharpe, made extensive use of the Bible, but he seemed to have regarded himself more as a political leader than as a prophet. The movement he organized did not aim to establish a new world, but to make specific and limited changes in Jamaican society; the slaves were to establish their right to sell their labor for wage.*[6]

It was not merely fortuitous then that Sam Sharpe, a church leader, provided the political leadership for this Revolt. This ideological tradition of understanding the Sam Sharpe Revolt as a political act is underscored by Michael Manley, whose government was responsible for making Sam Sharpe one of Jamaica's National Heroes, when he declared the Sam Sharpe Revolt as a 'reminder that no society is worth surviving which is not based on human dignity, freedom and justice.'[7] Accordingly, 'he, [*Sharpe*] helped politicise that culture at a moment of crisis; organizing the slaves in a way which surely helped prepare them for the emancipation that soon followed.'[8]

What is striking about the Revolt is that it represents the practice of relating ideas to a social and political reality. Philip Gilbourne expresses his view of Sharpe thus:

> *Samuel Sharpe was a man with the intelligence and imagination to put ideas into motion, putting together a set of related concepts based upon the right of every human being to freedom and dignity; bowing the knee to neither white tyrants, black tyrants, brown tyrants, or any other kind of tyrants. Bowing only to a God of Goodness, Love and Justice.*[9]

Gilbourne's comments on the political view of the Sam Sharpe Revolt, emphasizes the nature of the goal of the Revolt. This emphasis, however, is only one aspect of the Revolt.

Industrial Action

The other dimension of the political perspective of the Sam Sharpe Revolt is the means that the Revolt sought to employ to accomplish its goal. The Revolt was a form of industrial action, a strike or refusal to work without a just wage.[10] Scholars came to this conclusion based on the testimony of Sharpe and his compatriots which they gave to the authorities and the missionaries. Henry Bleby, the British missionary supports this point of view in his account of their testimony of the Revolt:

> *The plan proposed to be acted by Sharpe was that of passive resistance, and to fight only in case the "buckras" used forced to compel them to work as slaves. He thought that if they all "sat down" and refused to go to work again in the capacity*

> *as slaves after Christmas, carefully abstaining from offering violence to any person, it would be a very difficult thing for the masters to force such an immense body of people to work against their will.*[11]

Fully aware that the Jamaican House of Assembly unilaterally changed the number of holidays from three to two, Sharpe responded with this ingenious plan. Sharpe devised the plan that since the enslaved had holidays on Sunday and Monday, they would not return to work on Tuesday without being paid for the day of work. The enslaved were entitled to two days off from work. It happened, however, that in 1831, Christmas Day fell on a Sunday; thus it was a rest day as well as a holiday to which they were entitled. It was therefore not a usual day off from work. As a result, they would not return to work on Tuesday unless they were going to be paid for it.

This strike or industrial action for wages, Frank Hill defines as 'The First-ever strike for wages in Jamaica.'[12] Historian Edward Braithwaite concurs with this perspective of the Sam Sharpe Revolt. He writes:

> *He [Sharpe] had come to recognize the economic importance of labor to the system at a time when slaves were not even recognized as labor, but as chattel/things; mindless, without hurts and dignity of their own.*[13]

Brathwaite recognizes the impact industrial action would have had on the social and political system. He supported this assertion with the startling claim that; His [*Sharpe's*] declaration, therefore that the organized slaves 'set down after Christmas' 1831 and do not work until the conditions of their labour were improved, were a revolutionary idea with great implications.[14] Indeed, in the context of the struggle for liberation, political actions can be revolutionary not only because they lead to the transformation of society but because they are counter-cultural. Brathwaite affirms this view of the Sam Sharpe Revolt arguing that it was to be 'carried out peacefully (except in self-defence) was equally momentous in a plantation world that until then knew little else than gun and whip, treadmill and shackle.'[15]

Arguing that Sharpe was Jamaica's first labour leader, Sam Sharpe scholar, C.S. Reid acknowledges Sharpe as one who did not just give lip service to workers' affairs. He defended his fellow workers.[16] In an address commemorating the 150th anniversary of the execution of Sam Sharpe, Reid is careful to make an important distinction between Sharpe and contemporary labour leaders. Reid argues that where the current worker or union/labour leader 'who goes on strike today, may lose his day's pay: his leader loses nothing. For Sam Sharpe calling a strike could mean him losing his head.'[17] Reid is careful to acknowledge that Sharpe was defending the workers' right but the Revolt transcended the local context to represent a strike against the social and economic system.

The Religious Perspective

The Sam Sharpe Revolt is also interpreted as a religious event. The mistaken and ill-informed conclusion, however, is that since the Revolt was carried out by Christians then that made it a Christian event. In calling attention to the different religious perspectives, it is to be understood, on one hand, that something can be religious but not Christian. While on the other hand, something cannot be Christian without being religious.

The possible solution to this seemingly disjuncture between the religious and the Christian perspective resides in the urgent need to clarify the meaning of these terms. The suggestion here is that this distinction in grasping the meaning and significance of the Sam Sharpe Revolt cannot be separated from the religious character of the event. The religious perspective might be defined as a hermeneutic that does not deny a materialist interpretation of history, yet endeavours to explain historical forces as operating through social categories which possesses and establishes their own essential mechanism of operation.

From such an approach, the Sam Sharpe Revolt is more than it appears to be. The Revolt as an act against oppression may constitute certain essential religious elements but its theological dimension must not be overlooked. The religious perspective therefore, is the recognition of the empirical understanding of the Revolt but equally important is the involvement of the Divine in human history.

Behind these concerns is the fact that while the religious perspective understands the Revolt as reflecting a religious character and motivation, the event, nevertheless, has two different religious interpretations, one a Moslem interpretation and the other a Christian interpretation.

Moslem Interpretation

Sultana Afroz of the University of the West Indies advances the Moslem perspective by arguing that the Revolt is erroneously interpreted as a 'Baptist War.' It was rather a Moslem Jihad, a religious holy war, against oppression, which in this case, is against slavery. She establishes her perspective on three primary factors; namely the number of Moslems who constituted the large number of Africans whom the Europeans enslaved and transported to the Caribbean, particularly to Jamaica; the issuing of a Pastoral Letter calling for a religious war against the oppression of slavery and the recorded testimonials of the faith of the enslaved.[18]

The claim is that the human beings the European slave traders transported to the Caribbean as slaves originated mainly from West and Central Africa where Islam was the dominant religion. In Afroz's view, not only was Islam the dominant religion long before the Atlantic Slave Trade began, but these enslaved people were mostly members of the intellectual class such as the merchants, scholars, leaders and students.[19]It indicates that this sector of the enslaved community provided the religious leadership.

Assuming that Afroz's claim is correct, her observation reveals deep insights into the nature of the religion of the enslaved. But since she has not demonstrated that Islam had indeed been the major religious influence in this area of Africa, her claim should be taken as an educated speculation. Moreover, Afroz has not taken into account the fact that traditional African religions were the dominant religion in West African prior to the period of the Atlantic Slave Trade. It could then be argued that Afroz is reading into the evidence rather than reading from it; thus, undermining her claim.

Yet, there remains an alternative view. The enslaved were a religious people. Historian Dale Bisnauth, whose perspective of the Revolt is conflicting,[20] suggests the social context of the enslaved was not conducive to the development of their religion. For Bisnauth, the separation of the enslaved from each other, the inconvenience, lack of a central and stable place for worship, such as a mosque and other factors that are essential to religious life made it difficult, if not impossible, for the enslaved to practise their native or ancestral religions including Islam.[21]

Notwithstanding Bisnauth's contention, Afroz further establishes her claim based on the existing testimonials about and from the enslaved. These testimonies include interviews and historical writings, correspondences and autobiographical records of the enslaved. According to Afroz, these testimonials reveal that many of the enslaved were not only coerced into practicing the religion of the enslavers but were committed to their own religion by practicing it privately.[22] For Afroz, therefore, the enslaved practised Islam under the disguise of Christianity. She states:

> *The Abrahamic heritage of Islam and Christianity enabled the Moslem slaves to secretly practice Islam, while outwardly professing Christianity and maintaining membership of the local Christian churches...[but] this practice...seems to have been only a pretension adopted to avoid confrontation and punishments from the plantation owners and the church.*[23]

In this sense, Afroz is asserting that the foundation of the religion of the enslaved was Islamic but she does not provide any evidence to justify these claims which can equally be made for masking Traditional African Religions. In addition to their religious practices as noted earlier, Afroz believes the leaders including George Liele, Moses Baker, George Lewis and other African Americans[24] who helped to establish Black religion in the Caribbean and Sam Sharpe, the preacher and leader of the Revolt against slavery and others, were Moslems.[25] In this view, these Moslem leaders employed religious practices that were similar to those in Christianity, such as preaching, prayers, singing and meetings.[26]

Afroz's additional claim in interpreting the Sam Sharpe Revolt as an Islamic event is predicated on the issue of the 'Pastoral Letter' concerning a call for a religious war. She argues that this 'Pastoral Letter' originated in Africa and circulated among the enslaved in Jamaica. The call for war as the letter advocated concurs with the Islamic scripture which commands resistance to oppression. As Afroz correctly points out, 'The slave system of plantation Jamaica in its entirety was a symbol of evil and an instrument for safeguarding the privileges, ambitions and greed of the planters and a priestly class at the expense of the human dignity of the enslaved.'[27] In such a case, Islam was the motivating factor in the war waged by the enslaved against oppression and the quest to establish a society based on the values and principles of 'freedom, equity, justice, benevolence, compassion and wisdom'[28] similar to the Christian understanding of the Revolt as signified in the term 'Baptist War' or 'Christmas Rebellion.'

A problem arises, however, when we postulate such a claim on the basis of similarities between any two different realities. It seems that Afroz is reading the Sam Sharpe Revolt through Islamic lenses by defining it as an Islamic Jihad due to the commonalities with the 'Baptist War.' In this case, Christians could dispute her claim arguing that they are Christian practices. Moreover, arguing that the majority of the enslaved who came to the Caribbean were Moslems who used Christianity as a disguise for practising their religion, suggests that they were Moslems in Christian clothes. One can wonder nevertheless, what would be Afroz's response to the claim that such practice is Islamising Christianity. Despite the fact that she observes that these Moslems were devoted to Allah and not Jesus Christ, her claim, however, contradicts the testimonies of the enslaved especially in the case of Sam Sharpe and George Liele as discussed in chapters one and five respectively. For example, Sam Sharpe is reported to have based his action on his faith in Jesus Christ. He stated: 'If I have done wrong in that, I trust I shall be forgiven; for I cast myself upon the Atonement...I depend for salvation upon the Redeemer who shed his blood upon Calvary for sinners.'[29] George Liele also defined himself as a Christian. He confessed in his personal testimony of faith that, '[*I*] saw my condemnation in my own heart, and I found no way wherein I could escape the damnation from hell, only through the merits of my dying Lord and Savior Jesus Christ... for the salvation of my immortal soul.'[30]

Notwithstanding this contradiction in Afroz's argument, one cannot deny that some of the enslaved were Moslems.[31] The reality that there were Moslems in Jamaica does not make the Sam Sharpe Revolt a Jihad. In fact, not all of the enslaved were Moslems given the fact that they came from a religious pluralistic society.[32] Still, how does Afroz account for the African-derived religions such as Myalism, the Native Baptists, Revivalism and so forth?[33] In light of her claim, it would also follow that the African-derived religions were also disguises for Islam. But this assertion is very unlikely given that there are no indications of the continuity of Islamic religious practices in Jamaica and whereas there is evidence of African-derived religions. Thus, this lack of continuity of Islamic religious practices undermined Afroz's theory of the Sam Sharpe Revolt as a Moslem religious war. As Dale Bisnauth notes; 'The religion [*Islam*] did not long survive the rigors of the Middle Passage and the plantation system...The plantation system which was geared exclusively to sugar production gave no scope for the development of Islam as the African village did.'[34]

There were, however, hostilities from the Euro-American Christians towards the religion of the enslaved Africans. African American theologian, Dianne Stewart, affirms this view. She differs, nonetheless, by asserting that while European Christianity opposed the African-derived religions of the enslaved, the enslaved created their own religion which they termed 'African-derived'[35] religions as mentioned above.

Christian Interpretation

The religious perspective of the Sam Sharpe Revolt also consists of a Christian understanding. The common belief about the Revolt attributed its cause to the non-conformist churches. This view defines the Revolt as a 'Baptist War' or a 'Christmas Rebellion'.[36] Although these terms are used to identify the Sam Sharpe Revolt, they are intended to be interpreted as referring to or describing the religious dimension of the Revolt from a particular Christian perspective. In this sense, the Revolt is regarded as a 'Baptist War' because its leadership and the majority of its participants were members of the Black or Native Baptist church.[37] In fact, while the other non-conformist churches such as the Methodist, Presbyterian and Moravian disassociated themselves from the Revolt,[38] these same non-conformist churches were accused and persecuted for instigating the Revolt. The local government of the time, held to the notion that the church caused the Revolt. For example, The Jamaican Assembly report of March 1832 unapologetically located responsibility on 'a mischievous abuse existing in the system adopted by different religious sects in this island, termed Baptists, Wesleyan Methodists and Moravians.'[39]

Baptists, however, were held as the primary instigators of the Revolt.[40] In the aftermath of the Revolt, the Baptist leaders such as William Knibb[41] and Thomas Burchell[42] supported the Revolt and joined the liberation struggle against slavery and oppression. The pro-slavery newspaper,

The Jamaica Currant published a letter indicating that Knibb and other members of the clergy were arrested because they were Baptists. The letter states:

> *The Baptist ministers, are now in custody and we are satisfied that they would not have been taken into custody upon slight powers by Sir Willoughby Cotton, we hope he will afford them fair and impartial justice. Shooting is, however, too honourable a death for men whose conduct has occasioned so much bloodshed and loss of so much property.*[43]

In defence of the plantocracy, the testimony of a witness is deeply revealing: 'I regard all missionaries as emissaries from those who wish to ruin the colony. The precepts of the Baptists, I am told, are more bloody; but all with heaven in their eyes and hell in their hearts seek our destruction.'[44] The remark of the Custos of St James, Richard Barrett, was more specific: 'The doctrines of the Baptist minister himself may have been free from intentional guilt, but nevertheless, may have been perverted by ill-disposed slaves to forward their malpractices.'[45]

William Knibb[46] and Thomas Burchell[47] as white clergy persons pastored churches where enslaved Africans constituted the majority of the membership. This suggests that they were leaders of a people who were denied freedom and at the same time their lives were grounded, shaped and guided by a religious tradition that symbolized freedom. The implication is that the accusers did not take into account that freedom is one of the essential characteristics of Christian theology in general and Baptist theology. Writing of this essential element in Baptist theology, historian Horace Russell observes that 'Baptists have over the centuries marched to a drumbeat of freedom.'[48]

Russell is suggesting by this helpful remark that there is a tradition of Baptists' involvement in the human struggle for liberation. He premised this assertion on the notion of freedom as a 'practical and experiential activity.'[49] It was this vision of freedom that inspired the Sam Sharpe Revolt. As Russell notes; 'because Baptists have always held freedom to be a human right, answers must be found. They believed the Gospel. And in that witness lies always danger.'[50] Russell's claim suggests that the notion of the Sam Sharpe Revolt as a 'Baptists War' or 'Christmas Rebellion' is not due to the denominational affiliation of its leaderships and participants but rather the theological perspective of the proponents. Thus, religious affiliation is secondary to the religious perspective of the Sam Sharpe Revolt. It further suggests that this Revolt as a religious event can be regarded as a practical expression of freedom. Such interpretation does not proceed from the view of the separation of the sacred from the secular but from a holistic theology.

Theological Perspective

In this regard, a third perspective, a theological interpretation of the Sam Sharpe Revolt is proposed. This perspective seeks to understand the Revolt in light of faith in Jesus Christ from the standpoint of the Black Atlantic experience. Theological perspective is discussed in greater details in chapter seven; nevertheless, it is important to define and delineate what is meant by the theological perspective of the Sam Sharpe Revolt.

Both Christians and Moslems interpret the event as a religious act but the religious and the political perspectives do not take into account the theological perspective. Yet, the theological perspective consists of both the political and religious.

Also, with the understanding of the Sam Sharpe Revolt as a political event, it is arguable that the enslaved had neither the military nor the economic power to fight against the oppressive system of government. Nevertheless, undeterred by such challenges, the enslaved used their faith as the basis and impetus to venture on an all-out attack on the system of slavery even if it meant losing their lives. In this regard, Clarence Reid writes: 'Surely it was Sam Sharpe's grasp of the deeper implications of the Christian Faith that made him conclude that though he broke unjust laws of his slave masters he would find forgiveness with God who had made him with the right to be FREE.'[51] As the theological perspective is the emphasis of this book, this stage of the discussion therefore provides an opportunity to define and develop the theological perspective in more detail.

Arguing that the Christian faith of the enslaved played a pivotal role in the Sam Sharpe Revolt is to demonstrate both its theological basis and character. For example, the enslaved expressed the view that the Revolt was not a mere human work but also the work of God.[52] It is in this sense that the Sam Sharpe Revolt is a theological act, doing God's will of liberation for the fullness of life. This perception of doing God's will is detected in Sharpe's own self-understanding of the Revolt as indicated in the speech Henry Bleby, the Methodist clergyman, reported that Sharpe delivered to his colleagues prior to the beginning of the Revolt. Sharpe expressed the theological basis of the Revolt in (a) the natural equality of all persons, (b) the natural right for freedom, (c) the authority of Scripture, and (d) the cultural observance of the African religious practice of 'taking the Oath' and 'Kissing the Book' as an act of covenanting to stand in solidarity with each other for their cause.[53] For instance, when he was asked about the basis and reason for the Revolt, Sam Sharpe responded by appealing to the authority of the Bible Witness[54] using claims such as 'No man can serve two masters…' (Matt. 6:24); 'If the Son therefore shall make you free, you shall be free indeed.'(John 8:36); 'Ye are bought with a price: be not ye servants of men' (1 Cor. 7:23).[55] This suggests therefore, that it was clear to Sharpe that the Biblical Witness both authorized and justified the Revolt.

Conclusion

It is clear that there are different perspectives or approaches to interpret and study the Sam Sharpe Revolt. Certainly, using the vocabulary of perspective implies normative understanding of diversity and implicitly an organic difference. This duality might be described as the tension between the status-quo and change. Still, this tension is part of our social and moral formation as well as part of a larger and longer history and heritage. It is in this context of conjectural analysis that we can understand the Sam Sharpe Revolt as not only a complex, multi-dimensional, socio-political event but as a relentless theological act.

Thus, the ideas discussed in this chapter do not provide a blueprint for political action or solutions to problems faced by the Black Diaspora, people of African heritage, due to slavery, colonialism, capitalism and globalization. Instead, they are intellectual tools for interpreting the Black Atlantic experience. Pertaining to the Sam Sharpe Revolt, it is a paradigm of this Black experience in light of the God who is revealed in Jesus Christ.

The theological discourse that must transcend the reach of the geographically defined manifestations (African American, Black British and Caribbean) of Black theology, to address the common concerns and challenges of our time. Any such discourse must consider the social context and historical factors that help to define and produce this theology. Exploring this context is the subject of the next chapter.

Notes

1. Henry Bleby, *Death Struggle of Slavery* (London: Hamilton, Adams and Co., 1853), 113.
2. Mary Turner, *Slaves and Missionaries: The Disintegration of Jamaican Slave Society, 1787–1834* (Kingston: University of the West Indies Press, 1998), 148–78; Rupert Lewis, 'Sam Sharpe,' the *Sunday Gleaner*, 6 January 1980.
3. Michael Craton, *Testing the Chains: Resistance to Slavery in the British West Indies* (Ithaca: Cornel University Press, 1982), 291; Winston Lawson, *Religion And Race: African and European Roots in Conflict - A Jamaican Testament* (New York: Peter Lang Publishing, Inc., 1996), 150–85.
4. Hilary McD. Beckles, 'Caribbean Anti-Slavery: Self-Liberation Ethos of enslaved Blacks' in *Caribbean Slavery in the Atlantic World; A Student Reader*, ed. Verene Shepherd and Hilary McD. Beckles (Kingston: Ian Randle Publishers, 2000), 869.
5. Edward Braithwaite, 'The Anatomy of the Slave Revolt,' *Jamaica Historical Society Bulletin* 8 December, (1981): 80–95.
6. Mary Reckford, 'The Jamaica Slave Rebellion of 1831,' *Past & Present*, 40 (July, 1968): 108–24.
7. Michael Manley, 'Nanny, Sam Sharpe helped set road to freedom,' the *Jamaica Gleaner*, 19 October 1975.
8. Edward Brathwaite, *Wars of Respect: Nanny and Sharpe and the Struggle for People's Liberation* (Kingston: Agency for Public Information, 1977), 29.
9. Philip Gilbourne, 'Two faces of Sam Sharpe,' *Sunday Gleaner*, 13 August 1982.
10. Bleby, 112–13.
11. Bleby, 113.
12. Frank Hill, 'Sam Sharpe led first strike in Jamaica for wages,' *Sunday Gleaner*, 26 October 1975.
13. Brathwaite, (1977), 25.

14. Ibid.
15. Ibid.
16. C. S. Reid, 'Sam Sharpe Lauded as Jamaica's First True Labor Leader...' *Star Western Bureau*, 24 May 1982.
17. Reid, 'Sam Sharpe Lauded as Jamaica's First True Labor Leader.'
18. Sultana Afroz, 'The Jihad of 1831–1832: The Misunderstood Baptists Rebellion in Jamaica.' *Journal of Moslem Minority Affairs*, 21, no. 2 (2001): 227–43. For an alternative perspective, see Maureen Warner-Lewis, 'Religious Constancy and Compromise among Nineteenth Century Caribbean Based African Muslims,' *Journal of Caribbean History*, 37: 2 (2003): 294–336; 'Jamaican's Muslim past: disconnecting theories.' *Sunday Gleaner*, 20 October 2002.
19. Afroz, 228.
20. Dale Bisnauth, 'The 1831–32 Jamaica Slave Revolt: The Case For A Holy War,' *Caribbean Journal of Religious Studies*, 21:1 (October, 2007): 28–44. In this article, Bisnauth argues that the Sam Sharpe Revolt is a Holy War but in an earlier work, *History of Religions in the Caribbean*, he discounted such claim. It would have been helpful if Bisnauth had admitted his change in perspective. This would at least, grant some measure of credibility to his latest perspective. Without some form of clarification as to the change in his perspective, Bisnauth's claims remain unclear and uncertain. In fairness to Bisnauth, however, he concluded that the Moslem perspective of the Sam Sharpe Revolt is an initial step of research in this area of theological discourse.
21. Dale Bisnauth, *History of Religions in the Caribbean* (Kingston: LMH Publishing Limited, 1989), 82–83.
22. Afroz, 228.
23. Afroz, 231. The hostility of Christianity towards the religion of the enslaved that Afroz is suggesting is unclear if this had anything to do with Islam. The evidence and understanding in this regard, concerns the African-derived religions such as Myalism, Revivalism, etc. I am wondering if Afrox is taking the attitude of the established church towards the religion of the enslaved and applying it to the claim of their Islamic religion. For an insightful study on the attitude of the European Christianity towards religion of the enslaved, see Dianne Stewart, *Three Eyes For the Journey: African Dimension of the Jamaican Religious Experience* (New York: Oxford University Press, 2005), 69–89.
24. Braithwaite, (1977), 20.
25. Afroz, 231–40.
26. Philip Sherlock & Hazel Bennett, *The Story of the Jamaican People*,

(Kingston: Ian Randle Publishers, 1998), 200–7.

27. Afroz, 234.
28. Afroz, 23.
29. Bleby, 118–19.
30. George Liele, 'Letter from George Liele to Dr John Rippon,' *Baptist Register,* 18 December 1791. For an introductory account of George Liele, see Edward A. Holmes, 'George Liele: Negro Slavery's Prophet of Deliverance.' *Baptist Quarterly* 20 (1963–4): 340–61; Perspectives of Liele as Christian, consult Clement Gayle, 'George Liele: Jamaica's First Black Preacher,' *Jamaica Historical Society Bulletin* 88 (1983): 199–215; Beverley Brown, 'George Liele: Black Baptist and Pan-Africanist 1750–1826,' *Savaco* (1975): 58–71.
31. Bryan Edwards, *The History, Civil and Commercial of the West Indies 1819*, Vol. 2 (New York: AMS Press, 1966), 71–72.
32. Albert Raboteau, *Slave Rebellion: The Invisible Institution in the Antebellum South* (New York: Oxford University Press, 1978): 1–42.
33. Dianne Stewart, *Three Eyes For the Journey: African Dimension of the Jamaican Religious Experience* (New York: Oxford University Press, 2005); Also see, Jean Besson, *Martha Brae's Two Histories: European Expansion and Caribbean Culture Building in Jamaica* (Chapel Hill: University of North Carolina Press, 2002; Kingston: Ian Randle Publishers, 2003), 239–76.
34. Bisnauth, 82–83.
35. Robert Stewart, *Religion and Society in Post Emancipation Jamaica* (Knoxville: University of Tennessee Press, 1992); 91–187; Another excellent study on Black Diasporan religion is, Joseph M. Murthy, *Working the Spirit: Ceremony of the African People* (Massachusetts: Bacon Press, 1994).
36. Craton, 293; For a perspective of the Sam Sharpe Revolt as a Baptist War, see G. A. Catherall, *Baptist War and Peace,* (Ph. D. Thesis, University of Hull, 1990).
37. Bleby, 112.
38. Hope Waddell, *Twenty-nine Years in the West Indies and Central Africa; A Review of Missionary Life and Adventure 1829–1858* (London: T. Nelson & Son, 1863), 51–69.
39. The Jamaica Assembly's report. *British Sessional Papers, Common, Accounts and Papers,* 1831–32, XLVII (561), 3.
40. Shirley C. Gordon, *God Almighty Made Me Free: Christianity in Preemancipation Jamaica* (Bloomington & Indianapolis: Indiana University Press, 1996), 97–109. For an account in defence against the

charge of instigating the Revolt, see T. Oxford, ed., *Colonial Slavery; Defence of the Baptists Missionaries from the charge of Inciting the Late Rebellion in Jamaican a Discussion between Rev. William Knibb and Mr P. Borthwick* (London: The Tourist Office, 1832). See also, *Facts and Documents connected with the Late Insurrection in Jamaica and the Violations of Civil and religious Liberty arising out of it* (London: Holdsworth and Ball, 1832).

41. Philip Wright, *Knibb The 'Notorious' Slaves' Missionary, 1803–1845* (London: Sidgewick and Johnson, 1973), 56–133.
42. William F. Burchell, *Memoir of Thomas Burchell,* (London: Benjamin L. Green, 1849), 173–287. For a perceptive account of the radicalism of Thomas Burchell, see G. A. Catherall, 'Thomas Burchell: Gentle Radical,' *Baptist Quarterly* 21: 8 (October, 1966): 349–63.
43. *The Jamaica Currant, 6* January 1832.
44. *British Parliamentary Papers Evidence of H.R. Wallace,* No, 561, 1832. Vol. XLVII, 188.
45. Ibid., 187, 188.
46. T. Oxford, *Defence of the Missionaries,* 6. Here Knibb stated the number of people, 983 who were members of his congregation but he did not say if this was one or more churches which constituted a circuit system. This membership was drawn from seven different plantations.
47. Burchell, *Memoir of Thomas Burchell.* For a refreshing account of this issue, see Fred Kennedy, *Daddy Sharpe: A Narrative of the life and Adventure of Samuel Sharpe, a West Indian Slave Written by Himself, 1832* (Kingston: Ian Randle Publishers, 2008), 195–292.
48. Horace Russell, 'Baptist and Liberation,' *Baptist Quarterly: Journal of the Baptist Historical Society,* XXX111, no. 7 (July, 1990): 326–30.
49. Russell, 328.
50. Russell, 329.
51. C. S. Reid, *Samuel Sharpe: From Slave to National Hero* (Kingston: The Bustamante Institute of Public and International Affairs, 1988), 103.
52. Great Britain Parliamentary Papers, *'Confession of R. Gardner,'*(no. 285), 1831–32.
53. Bleby, 111–12.
54. Bleby, 116; For a discussion on the Bible as not only Sharpe's basis of authority for the Revolt but also the Native Baptist resistance against oppression particularly in the case of the Morant Bay Rebellion, 1865, see Devon Dick, *The Cross and the Machete: Native Baptists of Jamaica – Identity, Ministry and Legacy* (Kingston: Ian Randle Publishers, 2010), 100, 136–37.
55. C. S. Reid, (1988), 60.

3 - Living in Buckra's House: The Making of a Liberator

INTRODUCTION

This chapter attends to the social context of the society in which Sam Sharpe lived by examining the factors that shaped his life. In studying theology, especially Black theology, one becomes increasingly aware of the relationship between social context and theology.[1] Exploring the social context allows theology to delve into social reality in order to excavate a faith that informs and inspires liberation. The discussion in this chapter, however, is not a history of the era but rather an examination of the social context in which Black religion and Euro-American Christianity encounter each other and the implications of this encounter for Black theology.

The nature and task of Black theology is not a preoccupation with abstract concerns but rather a radical engagement of discerning God's purpose as it relates to human liberation.[2] Theology that is understood as liberation regards social context as a text for discovering and learning about the revelation and involvement of God in human history. This assertion is predicated on the notion that social context is a text where God's revelation is taking place.[3] Social context as text can be understood as a contemporary 'scripture' of God's revelation in history. So, affirming social reality as a means of Divine revelation requires one to listen to this reality in order to discern and construct the theology that emerges out of it. Thus, theology in this sense is not a declaration from God but critical reflection on the encounter between the Divine and human beings in light of the life, teachings, death and resurrection of Jesus Christ.

Since theology emerges out of a social context, what then are the social realities that provide insights for theological discourse on the Black experience? More specifically, what are the factors that shape and define the life of Sam Sharpe in which the theology of liberation becomes praxis? In answering these questions, three representative factors are identified that can be interpreted to characterize the society in which Sam Sharpe lived and which contributed to making him into a liberator. These characteristics, which are considered in turn are, the plantocracy into which he was born, the culture of resistance from which he came and the religion he practiced.

The Plantocracy

The life of Sam Sharpe is to be understood within the institution of slavery but it is situated within the particular context of the plantation system. Since Sharpe lived not only in slavery but on a plantation, any understanding of his life therefore must take into account this particular system that characterized his social context.

The plantation system was part of the global institution of slavery. The term plantation refers to the practice of owning land and human beings in the pursuit of wealth and power. More precisely, the plantation is 'a unit of land-holding and people-holding, each plantation a microcosm of colonization and each colony in turn shaped by this newly defined plantation.'[4]

Another characteristic of the plantation system is conflict. Conflict is the interplay of a dynamic combination of diverse forces such as restriction of movement and the desire to be free, segregation and the need for community, poverty and suffering. Historians Philip Sherlock and Hazel Bennett advance this view of the social character and ethos of the plantation system. They write:

> *Every aspect of the plantation represented conflict: black slave and white master, slave masters and great houses, provision ground and plantation, outlawed religions cults and established church, justice for whites and legally instituted injustice for blacks, chattel status for blacks and civil rights for whites, restricted movement for blacks and freedom for whites, pickney gangs for blacks and schools for whites, the 'bongo image' against the 'busha image,' yard-talk and English, slave and freeman [person].*[5]

This complex dichotomous society reflects the nature of the daily existence of the enslaved. They had to contend with these harsh realities without allowing them to define their identity or determine their destiny. Helping us to understand the complex nature of this system is B. W. Higman in his two excellent works, *Montpelier Jamaica: A Plantation Community in Slavery and Freedom, 1739–1912* and *Plantation*

Jamaica, 1750–1850. These works provide a reconstructive account of the plantation system attending to the issues of ownership and internal structure but points to the dialectical yet conflicting relationship between power and powerlessness. For Higman, ownership refers to the institution of power which controlled the natural, productive and financial resources of the country. The internal structure concerns the organization and management of the system in question.

Although Higman does not provide an ideology of the plantation system, he however identifies five of its definitive factors: namely, a place of identity, laboratory of autonomy, source of income for Western enterprises, absence of central leadership and diversified economy.[6] In this sense, the plantation system is a combination of complex and conflicting social factors that define the context in which Sharpe lived. Thus, in Sam Sharpe becoming a liberator, the plantation as a place of identity and a laboratory of autonomy may be interpreted as playing a central role.

Place of Identity

The place of identity interprets the plantation in terms of its physical and social location. This was the space that shaped the geography, constructed the municipality and defined the identity of the plantation as a particular social entity of people of common origins, life and interests.[7] This feature is crucial in that it shows how the enslaved were used to develop communities and the geographical landscape of the society. Philip Sherlock and Hazel Bennett in their book, *The Story of the Jamaican People* have identified this important characteristic. They note: 'Layout was important. The principal objectives were a central location for the works and an overall symmetry in ordering of building and crops.'[8] In the modern era, many people have a choice as to where they live; however, for the enslaved living in colonial plantation societies, there was definitely no such luxury. For example, the enslaved were either sold or hired as the slave holders desired.

In his book, *Daddy Sharpe,* Fred Kennedy provides an eloquent literary account of this inhumane practice. In this novel, Kennedy describes a dialogue between Sharpe and his master as a complex interplay between the powerful and the powerless which, theologically understood, displays the dialectical relationship between predestination and free will (Rom. 9:1–33). Sharpe's master decided that he would not sell him to anyone but he would hire him out to an estate owner. Sharpe did not want to leave the place which he regarded as his home but obviously, he had no choice in the matter. Kennedy describes the event this way.

> *I have decided that it is best for all of us that, Sam, I hire you out elsewhere so that you may take leave from Cooper's Hill. I have made arrangements with a lady by the name of Miss Garcia of Montego Bay...I had considered making some provisions for your manumission, but in light of the circumstances, I will postpone the plan...Miss Garcia is prepared to pay handsomely for you...but I chose to keep ownership of you for the time being...*[9]

Here Kennedy reveals not only the enormous power of slaveholders but the conditions under which the enslaved lived. As Higman puts it:

> *In slavery, people have very little or no choice in their employers, their sites of labor their tasks, their hours and days of work their conditions of labor, their food, clothing, and shelter. They were beaten and abused.*[10]

Although the enslaved did not have any choice regarding their geographic and social locations, the conversation between Sharpe and his so-called owner depicts the social fabric of the plantation. Also, Kennedy's portrayal of Sharpe's reaction to his sudden separation from his 'home,' continued exploitation of his service and ubiquitous disdain for Black humanity, reflects a self-understanding and affinity rooted deeply in a particular social context: He notes: 'My departure from Cooper's Hill was sudden...I did not know then if I would ever see my childhood friends, my master and mistress again. And so it was that Bay became my place of residence.'[11]

Place of Autonomy

Along with a place of identity, autonomy is another definitive factor of the plantation system during the time of Sam Sharpe. In that society, the enslaved had their own social and economic system. This was a social and commercial gathering during their so called 'holidays.' They met on these occasions not only for socialization but at their 'Sunday Market' to purchase from and to sell their products to each other.[12] For instance, Fred Kennedy calls attention to this essential practice in his imaginative interpretation of the life of Sam Sharpe. He writes of Sharpe's sense of freedom, joy and experience in going to the market: 'The Bay fascinated me. I visited stores where the dry-goods merchants sold cheese, ham, tea, port, and other wares like boots and saddles. I loved watching people of all colours mingling like this.'[13] Kennedy seems to be involved in every aspect of Sharpe's life during this experience. He describes Sharpe soaking in every moment of his personal freedom:

> *I enjoyed the errands Miss Mary sent me on because I was able to leave the house to go into the Bay... Early Sunday morning in the Bay, Barnet Street was lined up with slave women coming down from the mountain, balancing on their heads big baskets full of fruits, vegetables, rum sugar, salt anything they could grow in their provision grounds.*[14]

Kennedy wants to emphasize the reality of what he understands about the plantation system so as to demonstrate its structural dimension. The plantation system, however, was paradoxical. Operating within this system of oppression was a system of freedom. The plantation system was a source of income or the economic engine for Western capitalism and within this same system, an alternative economic system was also created and operated by the enslaved.[15] What this suggests is that the system which perpetrated oppression was at the same time, a system that nurtured or could be regarded as a laboratory for self-determination or autonomy. Autonomy, in this sense, means the fierce resistance to the brutality of oppression and the radical engagement to transform the existing social order in making possible the fullness of life – freedom, justice and equality.

Acknowledging that the plantation was limited in physical and social space, Higman urges that what 'happened there had a significance that transcended the tight boundaries of village, plantation and valley.'[16] In this sense, the plantation community was part of a much larger social and political system. But while Higman's work focuses on an individual plantation, a universal ideology undergirds his perspective. He states: 'I see the village [*plantation*] as an element in a larger system which can only be understood in its totality, as part of the Atlantic World.'[17]

In this view, Higman identifies the global nature of slavery. He recognizes that plantation slavery was not an isolated practice but it was related to a larger system of oppression. One could say that the plantation system was the localizing of a global system of oppression. Thus, while the Sam Sharpe Revolt was a local event and took place in a particular historical context, the Revolt not only illustrates the relationship between the particular and the universal or the local and the global, but was part of the larger cause of resistance to oppression thus locating the Revolt within the Black liberation tradition.

Culture of Resistance

Together with the plantocracy, a culture of resistance is another characteristic of Sam Sharpe's society which also contributed to making him into a liberator. Sharpe came from and lived in a culture that resisted slavery. Advancing this notion of resistance, historian Hilary McD. Beckles argues that the enslaved had a highly developed ideology of political consciousness that informed and undergirded their quest for liberation. He bases his claim on the tradition of slave revolts which he understands within the larger framework of global Black liberation.[18] Beckles identifies three stages of slave resistance which he defines as early plantation (1500–1750) where the plantation society was developing, mature plantation society (1750–1800) which consists of the declining dependence of slavery and the crisis in plantation slavery (1804–38) marked by the abolitionist movement and the Haitian Revolution.[19]

Although these stages of slave resistance have not received any systematic examination, Beckles argues that three forms of struggle characterized the resistance movement. These forms of struggle include daily resistance as an attempt to hasten the day of liberation, failed plots with a reformist agenda and the successful revolution such as the Maroon Wars and the Haitian Revolution[20] and the Sam Sharpe Revolt. This notion of resistance underscores the belief that the enslaved neither accepted nor resigned themselves to slavery.[21] It attests to the accounts that the enslaved resisted prior to and during their journey from captivity to enslavement in the 'Middle Passage' (the transporting of captured Africans across the Atlantic Ocean to Europe, the Americas and the Caribbean) using various measures of resistance from running away, suicide to armed revolt.[22] For example, the Jamaican revolutionary leader and national hero, Nanny of the Maroons exemplified this culture of resistance. She organized and directed military campaigns against the British enemies and led her people with courage and determination in resisting oppression. As Caribbean historian Lucille Mair observes, 'of all the black resistance leaders of her time, Nanny was foremost among those who resolved never to come to terms with the English. She infected her followers with this determination, and their aggressiveness became legendary.'[23]

With this ideology of resistance, the enslaved, Beckles argues, 'wanted freedom by all means necessary or possible, and engaged in activities which ranged from self-purchase to violent armed struggle for territory and political sovereignty.'[24] In this respect, the culture of resistance is an essential element of Black experience indicating that the enslaved had their philosophy of freedom which is the belief that they were born free and had the right to achieve it through any means necessary. A well known song of the enslaved, 'The Song of the Eboes' powerfully illustrates their philosophy of freedom:

> *God almighty thank ye, God almighty thank ye!*
> *God almighty make me free.*
> *Buckra in this country no make we free.*
> *What Negro for do? What Negro for do? Take force by force!*
> *Take force by force!*[25]

This song reflects the fundamental ideology of slave resistance. This is an ideology formulated to achieve freedom. Verene Shepherd, for example, argues that the resistance activism of the Maroon and revolutionary of Jamaica, Tacky, who led the 1760 revolt against the British, can be regarded as the model of this ideology of cultural resistance. She regards the resistance struggle that Tacky led against British imperialism during the eighteenth century to have been part of the larger Black struggle for liberation. Shepherd also acknowledges that the Tacky Revolt has inspired other resistances and stands as a legacy of the quest for freedom. As such, the spirit of the resistance not only lives on today but sets in motion future liberation struggles.[26] Additionally, based on the accuracy of the most recent historical records, there have been a series of resistance struggles culminating into the Sam Sharpe Revolt of 1831–32.[27] This included the revolt of 1766 and 1777 where between 33 and 45 people of African descent were executed, the Second Maroon War in 1796[28] and the Argyle War in the parish of Hanover where properties were destroyed and an unknown number of those convicted were executed by the British.[29]

Although Beckles's notion of resistance describes the ideological framework of Sam Sharpe's society, one can wonder, however, if this ideology is limited to internal resistance such as oppositions and revolts and not to socio-political transformation of the society. For Beckles, resistance concerns the subjects remaining in the system of oppression but not changing or transforming it. The Maroon Wars and communities are examples of this practice. Maroons were the enslaved who escaped from the plantations to form their communities[30] usually in the mountainous areas of their respective country where they were not as vulnerable to attacks and recapture by the British. Surely, they opposed and revolted against the oppressive system of slavery, but never transformed the society.[31] Rather they were only interested in securing their own freedom. Once they were free, they cooperated with the oppressors in maintaining the system of oppression by seeking and returning their fellow sisters and brothers into oppression.[32] This was the agreement they made with the government in order to secure and maintain their own freedom and community.

Clearly, the Maroons represent the Black struggle for freedom. Their isolationist practice, however, does not reflect the revolutionary dimension of revolt. In reality, the Maroons became a 'nation within nation.' One may wonder, however, if this form of resistance should not have been executed within the larger context of the oppression to indicate that resistance is part of a cause larger than and beyond the local and immediate context.

An example of the revolutionary dimension of resistance is demonstrated in the role of enslaved women in their struggle for freedom. Resistance represented a way of life for the enslaved. As such, this view questions any male-oriented interpretation of the culture of resistance. This point of view is delineated in Caribbean Women Studies. Barbara Bush, in her book, *Slave Women in Caribbean Society 1650–1838* pays close attention to the role of women in the struggle against slavery in Caribbean society while acknowledging their exclusion from the 'canon' of Black Freedom Fighters. Pointing out that it is not possible to ignore women as integral entities in the struggle against slavery, Bush provides a descriptive account of slave resistances consisting of two dimensions – individual and collective. She also argues that 'the unifying thread of the individual and the collective dimensions of resistance, is the African cultural heritage of the slave woman which fired her rebellious spirit, frequently bringing her into conflict with the laws and values of the master-class.'[33]

Certainly, the role of women is integral to the culture of resistance. Women played different roles including revolt leaders, providers of food, activists and so forth. As activists, enslaved women used the legal system to obtain whatever rights they had. These rights included having proper clothing, adequate food supplies, limited working hours, designated time off from work and maternal leave. Whenever these rights were violated, enslaved women, although they knew of the odds that were against them, brought charges against their plantation owners. For instance, some enslaved women brought charges before the court against their enslavers who may have flogged them more than what the law allowed. Lucile Mair in her book, *The Rebel Women in the British West Indies During Slavery* offers this powerful insight about the activist role of women in the culture of resistance.

> *By refusing to accept slavery like dumb animals, by regularly raising their voices, women, in their way, forced their presence on the consciousness of many: this was the thin end of the wedge in undermining the system of slavery. For once the slave is seen and heard as a human being, it becomes increasingly difficult to justify his or her existence as chattel.*[34]

Verene Shepherd helps to advance this perspective of the culture of resistance by arguing that women are constitutive element of this culture of resistance.[35] She identifies some of the women, such as Eliza Lawrence, Kitty Scarlet, Ann Guy and many others who played leading roles as protesters, strategists and supporters of the Sam Sharpe Revolt of 1831–32 but who were not as recognized as the men.[36] According to Shepherd:

> *These unsung female activists, equally submerged within the*

> *historiography, are not accorded the role of heroines of that momentous event. As in the conquests, colonization and decolonization, they were all male, in the treatment of resistance and revolts, women appear equally trapped in, and influenced by, a hegemonic gender-power relation of patriarchy.*[37]

It goes without saying that this view expresses the notion that resistance is not grounded in female or male essentials. Indeed, Shepherd's call to attend to the role of women in the struggle for liberation makes a difference in our understanding of the culture of resistance. Her call affirms the claim that it was both women and men who created the intellectual framework and were agents of this culture of resistance.

This advances the notion that resistance is concomitant to liberation. The culture of resistance is not merely an application of the idea of resistance or to join in a struggle but rather a commitment and participation in the struggle for human liberation and social transformation. As such, Sam Sharpe and his compatriots were more than products of, or shaped by, a culture of resistance but were both agents and embodiment of resistance.

With this understanding of resistance, resistance is interpreted as a theological act because the oppressed understands that to resist oppression is to do God's will for the realization of freedom. God willed freedom for all persons through Jesus Christ[38] but the enemies of Christ, such as slaveholders and wicked oppressors of human beings, opposed it through the maintenance of slavery and the perpetration of other oppressive ideologies and systems. As theologian James Cone reminds us, 'the meaning of Jesus Christ is found in God's will to make liberation not simply the property of one people but all humanity.'[39] Caribbean theologian Noel Erskine reinforces this claim by joining Cone in stating that: 'God became the freeing one who, even in the midst of human bondage, signaled to them that they were meant for freedom.'[40]

Religion of Liberation

In addition to the plantocracy and a culture of resistance, religion is the other factor that characterized the society and played a central role in making Sam Sharpe into a liberator. Conflict over and the demise of slavery marked the time of Sam Sharpe and religion was at the core of intensifying this conflict and hastening the demise of slavery. This issue, Mary Turner addresses in her important book, *Slaves and Missionaries.* Turner argues that the missionaries and the British abolitionists were in conflict over the issue of slavery. The missionaries wanted to Christianize the enslaved by teaching a one-dimensional Christianity. The emphasis of this kind of religion was the saving of the soul.

Religion from this perspective had no regard for the immediate reality of life such as the social and existential issues of life. Turner calls this version of religion 'missionary Christianity.'[41] The basis of this kind of Christianity can be summarized in the instructions that missionary agency such as the Baptist Missionary gave to those under their command.

> *You are quite aware that the state of society in Jamaica is very different from that under which it is our privilege to live in this country, and that the great majority of its inhabitants are dependent upon their superiors in a degree altogether unknown here. The evidences of the fact will probably, especially at first, be painful and trying to your feelings; but you must ever bear in mind, that, as a resident in Jamaica, you have nothing whatever to do with its civil and political affairs; and with those you must never interfere...*
>
> *The gospel of Christ, you will know, so far from producing or countenancing with a spirit of revolt or insubordination, has a directly opposite tendency...Let your instructions, both to the young and old, be conceived in a spirit, and, correspond with the directions and example, of our Divine Teacher, as laid down in the New Testament at large; and then whatever disposition may be felt to obstruct or misrepresent you, none will justly be able to lay anything to you charge.*[42]

This statement expresses the belief in the separation of faith from pubic life or the separation of the sacred from the secular. The Moravian church, for example, taught that slavery was not a sin. As such, they worked within the social political system without attempting to change it. Count Zinzendorf, the leader of the Moravian church expressed the belief that the enslaved should be content in their state and please their enslavers. In his view, God appointed some people to the status of a slave and some to the position of a master. As a result, he argued, 'Let us not demand to quit the position he has sent us to.'[43]

The Moravians were not the only church that held this view of slavery. As mentioned earlier, the Baptist held this view and also the Methodist[44] and Presbyterian churches. For example, the Presbyterian clergyman, Hope Waddell, echoes the stance of the church in this regard. In his failed attempt to prevent the Sam Sharpe Revolt from taking place, he reported that he urged the enslaved to 'prove their fitness for freedom by their continued good conduct; keep far from those who spoke of destroying either life or property; and especially sin not against the Lord.'[45]

Waddell's remarks represent his moral and theological basis not only for the enslaved to accept slavery but for the justification of the institution of slavery. Morally, the enslaved must prove that they were worthy of freedom. Theologically, the resistance of slavery was a sin. For Waddell, therefore, freedom is something that the enslaved must earn through the conformity to their condition and acceptance of the status quo. Also, his point of view reflects the belief that the enslaved were incapable of dealing with being free.

Waddell's claim, however, is morally and theologically inconsistent. On one hand, to revolt against slavery was a sin but on the other hand, he did not regard the practice of slavery as a sin. Unless Waddell was a supporter of slavery and did not regard the enslaved as human beings, how could he not see the contradictions between his so-called Christian faith and slavery? This failure of Waddell can be interpreted as the moral and theological inconsistencies of the church in relationship to the issue of slavery. In this regard, the established churches did not interpret slavery as a theological issue nor did they relate the Christian faith to social reality. Thus, for the Euro-American church at that time, sin was only personal and not social or systemic.

Unlike the 'established' church, Sharpe did not make this kind of distinction of sin regarding slavery. All he knew and believed was that it was not wrong to resist the oppression of slavery. As Bleby notes, 'he was not, however, to be convinced that he had done anyone wrong in asserting his claim to freedom.'[46] What this implies is that the society in which Sam Sharpe lived was in conflict between those who wanted to maintain the status quo and those who wanted to transform it based on religion.

Religion, therefore, not only intensified the conflict over slavery but also hastened its demise. Acknowledging the role of religion in the abolition of slavery, Mary Tuner advances the notion that the enslaved used Christianity as a means of securing their freedom and made the missionaries partners in their struggle for liberation from oppression.[47] Turner contends that the missionaries took a neutral position over the vexing and contentious issue of slavery. The Christianization of the enslaved was their purpose. This was the concern for the salvation of their soul without regard for their social conditions.[48] Writing in this regard, Oliver Furley notes:

> *Indeed, for many years it was urged that Christianising the slaves made them better slaves; the missionaries took pride in improving the system. The Christian slave was more diligent, more reliable and loyal, they pointed out.*[49]

For Turner, however, the enslaved used Christianity as a political tool to obtain liberation. She states that, 'The slaves transformed the missionaries' implicit message into action in the political circumstances created by the decade-long campaign for abolition of slavery launched in 1823.'[50] Turner in this remark is promoting the view that religion can play a political role accomplishing liberation from systemic and structural domination and oppression. For Turner:

> *Christianity became a political force when rumors of emancipation created political excitement...Political developments within the island had also broken whites exclusive monopoly of political power...[T]the Assembly was forced to concede the demands of the freed colored and black population in alliance with the imperial government for equal rights with the whites.*[51]

Turner is right in saying that religion can play a liberating role in society. Nonetheless, she interprets the Sam Sharpe Revolt as a political event without taking into account the theological basis of social action. It is here that historians and religious scholars exclude the role of faith in the Black liberation struggle. Turner for instance, points out that the missionaries regarded the cause of liberation from slavery as a humanitarian issue.[52] But it was not until the British abolitionists launched their formal campaign in 1823 against slavery that the missionaries were able to oppose slavery and so become involved in political engagement.[53] Writing in support of this assertion, Turner writes: 'The proliferation of Native Baptist sects was, therefore, a development full of political implications. The sects demonstrated that the slaves adopted the missionaries' religious teaching for their own ends.'[54]

Despite this important perspective, there is still an unanswered theological problem if we neglect to examine the role of faith in Black liberation. The liberation of the enslaved points to their faith and expresses their religion which Euro-American Christianity was determined to destroy through opposition, censorship and persecution.[55] Religious scholar Dianne Stewart succinctly summarizes this claim. Stewart states:

> *The missionaries assumed that Africans came to the Caribbean in a state of moral depravity and cultural barbarism. While many of them deplored slavery and believed the institution to be in contradiction with the gospel, they assumed cultural and religious superiority over Africans and saw themselves as endowed with the highest religious and cultural knowledges, which could save their inferior African brethren from sin and eternal damnation.*[56]

Clearly, the European missionaries failed to see the organic relationship between the religion of the enslaved and their quest for freedom. In fact, relating the Christian message of freedom to the condition of slavery was central to their liberation. Thus, without serious consideration of the centrality of faith in Black liberation, Turner's perspective of the demise of slavery promotes a one dimensional and non-theological view of Black liberation.

Departing from Turner's perspective, it can be contended that the faith of the enslaved was a resource they employed to secure liberation from slavery. Indeed, the enslaved understood their Revolt not only as applying their faith to the struggle for liberation from oppression but as doing the will of God (James 1:22–27). In fact, the enslaved believed they were 'assisting their brethren in the work of the Lord...

this was not the work of man [human] alone, but they had assistance from God.'[57] In this regard, the religion of the enslaved is both the evidence of their faith and a definitive factor of Sam Sharpe's society. Sharpe, therefore, rejected the religion that justified subjugation and oppression of any human being. He practised, instead, a religion of liberation for all persons. Sharpe made this clear when he said that 'he learned from his Bible, that the whites had no more right to hold black people in slavery than the black had to make the white people slaves.'[58]

Here, Sharpe underscored the collective belief of the equality of all persons as well as an essential element of his religion and faith. This affirmation of this element of Black Christianity reinforces the underlying theology of resistance that signifies departure from Euro-American Christianity. This departure, however, is not to be understood as rejection of Christianity but as an alternative to Euro-American version of Christianity. Gayraud Wilmore's study on Black religion affirms this claim. He observes:

> *Blacks have used Christianity not as it was delivered to them by segregated white churches, but as its truth was authenticated to them in the experience of suffering, to reinforce an ingrained religious temperament and to produce an indigenous religion oriented to freedom and human welfare.*[59]

The alternative to white versions of Christianity was the Black religion known as the Native Baptist. The term Native Baptist refers less to a religious group of Black Christians and more to an ideology of Black Christianity in the Caribbean.[60] The Jamaican Baptist clergywoman, Marvia Lawes, writing about Baptist spirituality of resistance, calls attention to this perspective. She writes:

> *...I am taking "nativism" to mean more than emerging out of the local context. In the case African Jamaicans who used the term Native Baptists, they are at least implied in their meanings Black or African in terms of ethnic roots.*[61]

Lawes uses the term to define the Black Christian tradition in Jamaica. This tradition originated from the work of the African American Christians such as George Liele, Moses Baker and George Gibbs,[62] who migrated to Jamaica after the American War of Independence in 1776.

In addition, this tradition of Christianity is defined by an African-derived cosmology, praxis and leadership.[63] In this case, the African-derived worldview constitutes the ideological framework of the Native Baptist.

The Native Baptist religion is the creation of Caribbean peoples.[64] It was organized by, consisted of and led by Blacks many years prior to the arrival of the European missionaries or the establishment of any Euro-American Christianity in Jamaica and the Caribbean.[65] Therefore, in organization, theology, membership and leadership, the Native Baptist religion was of African origin. Historian Shirley Gordon's study on the relationship between European Christianity and Black religion lends support to this claim. She argues that Black Christianity is the creation of Black enslaved believers. Gordon acknowledges that this version of Christianity was formed out of the religious beliefs and cultural values of the enslaved. Their faith, as a product and characteristic of this religion, formed the basis for their resistance and revolt against slavery.[66] Gordon concludes that the 'Native Baptist nevertheless adopted the desire for earthly freedom into their religious thought much earlier than the dissenting groups led by the British missionaries.'[67]

Gordon's observation can be interpreted as a demonstration of Black self-determination and willingness to embrace religion that accepts liberation as its essential purpose. For example, Sam Sharpe expressed this element of liberation by grounding the Revolt in his faith and in asserting the right to seek freedom[68] as discussed in chapter one with a further exploration in chapter five. Gayraud Wilmore in his important study on Black liberation affirms this assertion. He states:

> *They were fully aware that the God who demanded their devotion and the Spirit that infused their secret meetings and possessed their souls and bodies in the ecstasy of worship was not the God of the slave master with his whip and gun, nor the God of the plantation preacher with his segregated services and unctuous injunction to humility and obedience.*[69]

The distinct nature of the Christian religion which the enslaved created in the Caribbean is what is important. The Native Baptist religion was not a substitute for the European-centred religion but a religion that coexisted with this version of Christianity.[70] Sharpe may have maintained his relationship within the orthodox Baptist church, for what Shirley Gordon calls, respectability. In her view, these Black people embraced Christianity in order to become respectable in the society.[71] It is not clear if this was the case. What is certain, is that Sharpe was a member both of the Native Baptist church tradition[72] and the orthodox Baptist church tradition[73] as was discussed in chapter one. What this indicates, nevertheless, is that Sharpe belonged to and embodied a dialectical religious tradition[74] as will be explored in chapter four.

Conclusion

In this discussion on the social context of theological discourse, the discussion surrounds the Sam Sharpe Revolt as a paradigm to discern the theology that emerges out of this context. In the matrix of plantation slavery, the African-derived cultural milieu and Christian religious practice, we detect the emergence of Sam Sharpe as a liberator. The plantation system acted as supreme authority on earth, the African-derived culture provided the foundation for nurturing the ideology of liberation from oppression and for freedom, and the religion of the enslaved played an essential role to deploy the purpose of God for humanity. The result is the making of a liberator. Thus, it could be argued that the society nurtures those who become liberators as in the case of Sam Sharpe.

Sharpe was not only a product of his society but his work of liberation through his Revolt, was a sign of God's involvement in human affairs. What then emerges from this context is God's will of liberation for all persons. How this liberation is interpreted and appropriated is the discussion to follow.

Notes

1. James Cone, *God of the Oppressed* (New York: Seabury Press, 1975), 39–83. Cone's work represents the seminal text in this area of theological inquiry. As such, all subsequent study on this subject is not intented to refute this work of Cone. Both Caribbean theology and Black British theology stand in this theological tradition that Cone advocates. See for example, Lewin Williams, *Caribbean Theology* (New York: Peter Lang, 1994), 93–121; Robert Beckford's, *Dread and Pentecostal: A Black Political Theology for the Black Church in Britain* (London: SPCK, 2000), 208–20.

2. James H. Evans, Jr., *We Have Been Believers* (Minneapolis: Fortress Press, 1992), 3–10.
3. Delroy A. Reid-Salmon, *Home Away from Home: The Caribbean Diasporan Church in the Black Atlantic Tradition* (London: Equinox Publishing Ltd., 2006), 95–100.
4. B. W. Higman, *Plantation Jamaica 1750–1850* (Kingston: University of the West Indies Press, 2005), 5.
5. Philip Sherlock & Hazel Bennett, *The Story of the Jamaican People* (Kingston: Ian Randle Publishers, 1998), 151.
6. See B. W. Higman, *Montpelier Jamaica: A Plantation Community in Slavery and Freedom* (1998).
7. Higman, (1998), 1.
8. Sherlock and Bennett, 152.
9. Fred Kennedy, *Daddy Sharpe: A Narrative of the Life and Adventures of Samuel Sharpe, A West Indian Slave Written by Himself, 1832* (Kingston: Ian Randle Publishers, 2008), 122–23.
10. Higman (2005), 3.
11. Kennedy, 123.
12. Sherlock & Bennett, 172.
13. Kennedy, 125.
14. Kennedy, 125–26.
15. Sherlock & Bennett, 163–75; For an illuminating study on the internal market system, see Lorna Elaine Simmonds, 'The Afro-Jamaican and the Internal Market System, Kingston 1780–1834,' in *Jamaica in Slavery and Freedom: History, Heritage and Culture*, eds. Kathleen E. A. Monteith and Glen Richards (Kingston: University of the West Indies Press, 2002), 274–90.
16. Higman (1998), xii.
17. Ibid.
18. Hilary McD. Beckles, 'Caribbean Anti-Slavery: The Self-Liberation Ethos of Enslaved Blacks,' in *Caribbean Slavery in the Atlantic World*, eds., Verene Shepherd and Hilary McD. Beckles (Kingston: Ian Randle Publishers, 2000) 869–77.
19. Hilary McD. Beckles, 869.
20. Ibid.
21. Hilary McD. Beckles and Verene A. Shepherd, *Saving Souls: The Struggle to end the Transatlantic Trade in Africans* (Kingston: Ian Randle Publishers, 2007), 1–37; see also, Richard D. E. Burton, *Afro-Creole: Power, Opposition and Play in the Caribbean* (Ithaca: Cornel University Press, 1997), 47–89.

22. Richard S. Reddie, *Abolition: The Struggle to Abolish Slavery in the British Colonies* (Oxford: Lion Hudson plc, 2007), 110–24; For a case study on slave resistance, see Alvin O. Thompson, *Flight to Freedom: African Runaways and Maroons in the Americans* (Kingston: University of the West Indies Press, 2006), 91–144; Verene Shepherd, 'Women and the Abolition Campaign in the Africa Atlantic,' *Journal of Caribbean History,* 42:1 (2008): 131–53.
23. Lucille Mathurin Mair, *The Rebel Women in the British West Indies during Slavery* (Kingston: University of the West Indies Press, 2007), 50.
24. Beckles, 870.
25. 'The Song of the Eboes,' cited in Shirley C. Gordon, *God Almighty Make Me Free: Christianity in Preemancipation Jamaica* (Bloomington & Indianapolis: Indiana University Press, 1996), 54.
26. Verene Shepherd, *I Want to Disturb My Neighbour: Lectures on Slavery, Emancipation and Postcolonial Jamaica* (Kingston: Ian Randle Publishers, 2007), 73–80.
27. Shepherd, 75–80. For a detailed study of these resistance struggles, see Philip Sherlock & Hazel Bennett's, *The Story of the Jamaican People* (Kingston: Ian Randle Publishers, 1998), 133–49; 212–28.
28. Shepherd, 76.
29. Mary Turner, *Slaves and Missionaries: The Disintegration of Jamaican Slave Society, 1787–1834* (Kingston: University of the West Indies Press, 1998), 110–11.
30. Mavis C. Campbell, *The Maroons of Jamaica: A History of Resistance & Betrayal* (New Jersey: Africa World Press, Inc., 1990), 1–2.
31. Alvin O. Thompson, *Fight to Freedom: African Runaways and Maroons in the Americas* (Kingston: University of the West Indies Press, 2006).
32. Mavis C. Campbell, 126–63.
33. Barbara Bush, *Slave Women in Caribbean Society 1650–1838* (Bloomington: Indiana University Press, 1990), 52.
34. Mair, 25.
35. Shepherd, 132–36. I use this essay because it deals specifically with the Sam Sharpe Revolt. As such, I employ Shepherd's work in this instance not necessarily to represent but to illustrate the role of women in the struggle against slavery. For further enquiry, see Barbara Bush, *Slave Women in the Caribbean 1650–1838* (Bloomington: Indiana University Press, 1990), 51–82; Stella Dadzie, 'Searching for the Invisible Woman: Slavery and resistance in Jamaica,' *Race and Class,* 32. No. 2 (1990); Lucile Mathurin Mair, *The Rebel Woman in the British West Indies During Slavery* (Kingston: Institute of Jamaica for the African-Caribbean

Institute of Jamaica, 1975); Hilary McD. Beckles, 'Persistent Rebels: Women and Anti-Slavery Activity,' in *Caribbean Slavery in the Atlantic World*, eds. Verene Shepherd and Hilary McD, Beckles (Kingston: Ian Randle Publishers, 2000), 1001–16.

36. Verene A. Shepherd, 123–24; 133–25. See also, C. S. Reid, *From Slavery to National Hero*, 92–94.
37. Shepherd, 124.
38. James Cone, *God of the Oppressed* (New York: Seabury Press, 1975).
39. James Cone, 'Theology as the Expression of God's Liberating Activity for the Poor,' in *The Vocation of the Theologian*, ed. Theodore W. Jennings, Jr. (Philadelphia: Fortress Press, 1985), 121.
40. Noel Leo Erskine, *Decolonizing Theology: A Caribbean Perspective* (New York: Orbis Books, 1981), 1.
41. Mary Turner, 65–101.
42. Cited in Ernest A. Payne, *Freedom in Jamaica: Some Chapters in the Story of the Baptist Missionary Society* (London Carey Press, 1946), 21.
43. Cited in Oliver W. Furley, 'Moravian Missionaries and Slaves in the West Indies,' *Caribbean Studies* No. 5:2 (July, 1965): 3–16.
44. Henry Bleby, *Death Struggles of Slavery* (London: Hamilton, Adams and Co., 1853), 117. Bleby confronted Sharpe with the notion that the enslaved should be content in their situation and should leave any change of their condition to God. Bleby established his claim on the authority of Scripture but Sharpe did not accept such claim as a correct interpretation of the Scripture.
45. Hope Waddell, *Twenty-Nine Years in West Africa and the West Indies*, (London: T. Nelson, 1863), 52; See also, John Howard Hinton, *Memoir of William Knibb, Missionary In Jamaica (1849)* 2nd ed. (London: Houlston and Stoneman, 1896), 111–19.
46. Bleby, 117.
47. Mary Turner, *Slaves and Missionaries: The Disintegration and Jamaican Slave Society, 1787–1834.* (Kingston: University of the West Indies Press, 1998).
48. Turner, 65–94.
49. Furley, 15.
50. Turner, 91.
51. Turner, 149–50.
52. Turner, 102–31.
53. Turner 124.
54. Turner, 59.
55. Turner, 81.

56. Dianne M. Stewart, *Three Eyes for the Journey: African Dimension of Jamaican Religious Experience* (New York: Oxford University Press, 2005), 81–82.
57. Cited in Mary Turner, 155.
58. Bleby, 116.
59. Gayraud Wilmore, *Black Religion and Black Radicalism: An Interpretation of the Religious History of Afro-American people* (New York: Orbis Books, 1973), 5.
60. Dianne Stewart, xvi.
61. Marvia Lawes, 'An Historical Evaluation of Jamaica Baptists: A Spirituality of Resistance,' *Black Theology: An International Journal* (London: Equinox Publishing Ltd., 2008), Vol. 6 Number 3 366–92.
62. Shirley C. Gordon, *God Almighty Made Me Free: Christianity in Pre-Emancipation Jamaica* (Indianapolis: Indiana University Press, 1996), 41–55.
63. Lawson, *Religion and Race*, 4–150.
64. Dianne Stewart, 101–06. For a refreshing and informative study on this subject, see Robert J. Steward, *Religion and Society in Post-Emancipation Jamaica* (Tennessee: University of Tennessee Press, 1992), 110–52.
65. Clement Gayle, *George Liele: Pioneer Missionary to Jamaica* (Kingston: Jamaica Baptist Union, 1982), 3.
66. Shirley Gordon, (1996), 41–55.
67. Gordon, 53.
68. Bleby, 112.
69. Wilmore, 14.
70. Jean Besson, *Martha Brae's Two Histories: European Expansion and Caribbean Culture-Building in Jamaica* (Chapel Hill: University of North Carolina Press, 2002; Kingston: Ian Randle Publishers, 2003), 239–75.
71. Shirley C. Gordon, *Our Cause For His Glory: Christianisation and Emancipation in Jamaica* (Kingston: University of the West Indies Press, 1998), 120.
72. Mary Turner, 153.
73. C. S. Reid, *Samuel Sharpe: From Slavery to National Hero* (Kingston: Bustamante Institute of Public and International Affairs, 1988), 92–94.
74. Delroy A. Reid-Salmon, *Home Away From Home: The Caribbean Diasporan Church in the Black Atlantic Tradition* (London: Equinox Publishing Ltd., 2008), 60–75. I employ Sam Sharpe as a paradigm of the view that Caribbean Christianity is a dialectical religion as symbolized by Sharpe's membership in the African-derived Native Baptists and the Eurocentric Baptist Church Tradition. I am aware of

the discussion on creolization theory regarding this issue of 'dialect' especially the notion of dominance and/or mutuality. While the verdict is still out on whether the European religious tradition dominated the African or if both played a mutual role as constitutive elements of Caribbean Christianity, I propose that it is the essence of the religion which is definitive. In this case, liberation from oppression for freedom, justice and the fullness of life is the essence of Caribbean religion that Sam Sharpe practised and symbolized. For an introduction to Creolization theory, see Kamau Braithwaite, *The Development of Creole Society in Jamaica 1770–1820* (Kingston: Ian Randle Publishers, 2005) and his 'Caliban, Ariel, and Unprospero in Conflict of Creolisation: A Case Study of the Slave Revolt in Jamaica in 1831–32,' in *Caribbean Slavery in the Atlantic World*, eds. Verene A. Shepherd and Hilary McD. Beckles (Kingston: Ian Randle Publishers, 2000), 879–95. For a general analysis on Creolization theory, see Verene A. Shepherd and Glen L. Richards, *Questioning Creole: Creolisation Discourse in Caribbean Culture* (Kingston: Ian Randle Publishers, 2002); Rex Nettleford, *Mirror Mirror: Identity, Race and Protest in Jamaica* (Kingston: Collins and Sangster, 1970); Mervyn C. Alleyne, *Roots of Jamaican Culture* (London: Pluto Press, 1988); Orlando Patterson, 'Context and Choice in Ethic Allegiance: A Theoretical Framework and Caribbean Case Study,' in *Ethnicity: Theory and Experience*, eds., Nathan Glazier and Daniel P. Moynihan (Mass: Harvard Press, 1975), 319–34.

4 - Working in Vain: The Limits of Liberation

INTRODUCTION

In the wake of the revolt against the centrality of liberation in Black theology,[1] a distorted conforming version of this theology has emerged in theological discourse. Black religious experience has been chosen due to its prominence in Black intellectual and religious life as an example of this distortion of Black theology. This distortion of Black theology has also directed attention from the cause of liberation and has revealed further the marginalization of faith in Black theology. This is leading to what can be termed 'status-quo Black Christianity' which is defined as a non-transformative and non-prophetic practice of Christianity that conforms to the norms of the dominant society.[2]

Responding to this new trend to marginalize the role of faith in Black theology, it is argued in this chapter that it is a bold attempt to advance a theology of liberation without faith.

Liberation Without Faith

This notion of liberation without faith is the exclusion of the centrality of faith from Black theological discourse. Thus, the discussion in this chapter focuses on two components of a theology that excludes faith in Jesus Christ as liberator. The discussion begins with the de-centring of the Christian faith as a basis for liberation and concludes with the domestication of Black theology into status quo religious ideology.

The De-Centring of Faith

Beginning with the de-centring factor, the approach of Noel Erskine in his *From Garvey to Marley* and Dianne Stewart's, *Three Eyes for the Journey,* will serve as examples. Classical Black theology considers the church as an agent of liberation in the world.[3] Countering this claim, Erskine argues that liberation comes from outside the church because God operates outside the church and liberation is not confined to this one institution.[4]

He premises his argument on the idea that the 'established church' of the time was not concerned about the plight of the poor and was concerned only about middle-class interests. Arguing that this practice of the church reflects a colonized theology, Erskine proposes the decolonizing of theology which he interprets to mean doing theological reflection from the 'perspective of suffering and oppression' which Rastafarianism represents.[5] For Erskine, Rastafarian theology is a theology of liberation because it concerns the liberation of the poor[6] and is understood in relation to Africa.[7] This interpretation of Rastafarian theology, Erskine grounds in Black history including African and Caribbean history as resource for liberation.[8] Erskine emphasizes this aspect of Rastafarian theology because he considers it important that the concept of God is located in Africa and God is conceptualized and portrayed from the Black person's perspective. He expresses this point of view when he writes regarding the African identity of God in stating that 'locating God in Africa and pressing for an incarnational theology posits the blackness of God.'[9]

Erskine's view on the meaning of Africa, however, is not clearly defined. There is a distinction between continental Africa as a whole and West Africa from where the majority of the Black Atlantic Diaspora originated. If by Africa, Erskine means West Africa, which is only a geographical region that has come to define the people of African descent who are living outside the continent of Africa, then he generalizes the African identity. Erskine excludes the African origin of biblical Christianity[10] and fails to recognize that Christianity originated in Africa which persons such as Zephaniah (Zeph. 1:1),[11] St Augustine,[12] Athanasius[13] and others represent.[14]

The shift to Rastafarianism to demonstrate that liberation can be found outside the context of the church, however, is not a new practice in Black Christianity. Black people have established religions that express and promote a liberative self-understanding and practices. Randall Bailey calls attention to this phenomenon in writing that 'our fore-parents taught us that it is alright to change the story to be in line with our religious experience.'[15] Erskine acknowledges that this phenomenon can be seen in the Black religion of Myalism, Obeah, the Native Baptist, the United Negro Improvement Association of Marcus Garvey, as well as in events such as the Baptist War of 1831–32 and the Morant Bay Rebellion of 1838.[16] Erskine, nevertheless, understands these movements as alternatives to the church.

By arguing that these religions and movements operated outside the church, it could be argued that Erskine misinterprets the meaning of the church. These radical movements did not constitute the church but their work was that of expressing the Christian Faith in light of the existential realities of the time. In the case of the Morant Bay Rebellion, for example, both Paul Bogle and George William Gordon were deacons and therefore leaders of the church. These two leaders of the church regarded the social conditions of the country which included poverty, unemployment and other social ills as inhumane. Since the government was not willing to address the situation which Bogle and Gordon regarded as contrary to their faith and their view of God's will for the society, they responded in protest. In fact, Bogle and Gordon believed that their work of liberation was not only God's will but it was faith in God that inspired them to lead the protest. The following government report attests to this notion:

> *If a man like Bogle was in the habit of hearing such expressions as those contained in Gordon's letters as that the reign of their oppressors would be short, and that the Lord was about to destroy them, it would not take much to convince him that he might be the appointed instrument in the Lord's hand for effecting that end; and it is clear that this was Bogle's belief, as we find that after the part that he had taken in the massacre of Morant Bay, he, in his chapel at Stony Gut, returned thanks to God that he had gone to do that work, and that God had prospered him in his work.*[17]

While Erskine's claim that liberation is not the exclusive claim of Christianity is valid to some extent, he is confusing the Euro-American church or what Kelly Brown Douglas calls, 'Platonized Christianity'[18] with Black Christianity. Winston Lawson makes the distinction between these two conflicting religious traditions which he identifies as Black and Euro-American religions.[19] Writing of this distinction, Shirley Gordon suggests: 'From the mid-nineteenth century the development of Christian religion in Jamaica can be presented as a kind of counterpoint of movements in the two traditions which gave it birth.'[20]

Gordon's view suggests Black people created a church for themselves. This church was the birth of not only the Black church but the Black Church Tradition in the Caribbean. Recognizing the peculiar nature of this church, Jean Besson advocates the notion of the coexistence of two dominant religious traditions.[21] Although she agrees with Erskine that the church reneged on its role as an agent of liberation, she points out that the 'established church' of the society which was at the time, the Anglican church, did not appeal to the ordinary people of the society.[22] But Besson is careful to point out that the so-called 'Non-Conformist' churches such as the Methodist, the Moravian and the Baptist[23] had a greater appeal to the Black population due primarily to their interest in abolishing slavery.[24] It was the Baptist church, however, which was not only in the forefront of the liberation struggle but was also the church of and for the members of the Black community. As Orlando Patterson has observed, 'the slave[*s*] saw the Baptist missionaries [*church*] as their allies against the planters in their fight for freedom.'[25] The Black community used the Baptist denominational church as their formal religious organization, regarded the Baptist missionaries and clergy as comrades[26] in concert with their own African-derived religion as a counter-cultural source of protest and resistance.[27]

Notwithstanding this observation, the African and Euro-American religious character of Caribbean Christianity are not two conflicting religions but is rather one religion consisting of two dialectical religious traditions.[28] Probably, Erskine has failed to take note of the emergence of a distinct Caribbean Christianity that is represented, for example, in Jamaican Pentecostal religion.[29] This religion challenges Erskine's claim that the Christian church was not concerned about the plight of the poor. Pentecostalism is not only a religion of the masses which emphasizes personal piety, morality and sin as personal and not systemic, but is also a religion marked by its commitment to the poor and the marginalized.[30] In fairness to Erskine, Austin-Broos acknowledges the relationship between Pentecostalism and Rastafarianism. 'Both forms of religious practices operate in Jamaica with the assumption that earth-bound social relations are mediated by issues of race.'[31]

The other important supportive voice in the de-centring of the Christian Faith as a basis for liberation is found in Dianne Stewart's, *Three Eyes for the Journey.* The study is a liberationist interpretation of

Caribbean theology. She advances this argument that the Black people of the Caribbean created and have their own religion and distinct theology by examining the relationship between European Christianity and African-derived religions. Stewart gives particular attention to the nature of African-derived religions by delineating their theological commonalities based on a contextual interpretation of the cross from the perspective of womanist theology.[32] Stewart concludes with the view that African-derived religions are essential in defining the liberative dimensions of Caribbean theology.[33]

In concert with Erskine, Stewart argues that Rastafarianism rejects Christianity but also goes beyond this claim by indicting Christianity as an imperialistic religion. She is very suspicious of Christian theology because of both its imperialistic and elitist character. Stewart believes that Christian theology assumes itself to be normative for human faith and conduct based on the Christological confession of salvation for persons through the life of Jesus.[34] She promotes the notion that Myal, Obeah, Native Baptist, Revival-Zion, Kumina and Rastafarianism are examples of African-derived religions.[35] In Stewart's perspective, the claim of salvation through Jesus Christ is the reason for the impoverishment of Africa and people of African descent. This process, in which people are dehumanized, is known as 'anthropological poverty.'[36] Anthropological poverty strips people of their essence, identity and possessions.[37]

Dianne Stewart's piercing critique of the Caribbean Christianity must not remain unchallenged. She rejects the notion of Caribbean Christianity because of its Eurocentric character. Instead, Stewart accepts the notion of African-derived religions as the authentic Caribbean religion. For Stewart, African-derived religions are more than a religion of the African Diasporan people but they are also 'African religions in an oppressive New World.'[38] Stewart makes a distinction between the two sources of Caribbean Christianity by asserting that one is European-derived and the other African-derived. She understands these two religious traditions as opposing religions when Caribbean Christianity is made of two dialectical religious traditions. She writes: 'The missionary church competed with African religion in Jamaica and succeeded in forcing African practitioners underground and in stigmatizing African religiosity in the consciousness of its Christian converts.'[39] Stewart further suggests that Caribbean Christianity is European in 'theology, piety and consciousness.'[40]

Stewart's critique is sound in that the missionary church was anti-African, but the premise on which she constructs African-derived religions is a point of contention. She bases African-derived religions on the response of European Christianity which was hostile, oppressive and negative.[41] As a result of this negative response, Stewart proposes that African-derived religions provide an alternative religious agency for liberation.[42]

One can argue that these religions are also Caribbean religions. However, the African dimensions of Caribbean Christianity that Stewart defines as African-derived religions, is only one aspect of Caribbean religion. African-derived religions did not originate from Africa, Asia, Europe or any other region of the world except in the Caribbean. It is the product of what originates from the religious experience of the Caribbean people in their encounters with the various people who migrated to the Caribbean through the experience of slavery and colonialism. According to Robert Stewart in his resourceful book, *Religion and Society in Post-Emancipation Jamaica*, the product of this experience is what leads to the formation of Caribbean Church [*Black Church]*.[43] Thus, in response to Dianne Stewart's assertion of African-derived religions as an alternative agent of Black liberation, the view is maintained that Caribbean Christianity is an agency of liberation through faith as reflected in my interpretation of the Sam Sharpe Revolt.

Yet, observations should be made about this shift of the agent of liberation from the Christian religion to non-Christian religions. In considering the perspective of Noel Erskine as we have been discussing in this chapter, he attempts to construct a Black liberation theology by de-centring the Christian Faith as the agent of such discourse. However, he does so within a Christian framework. Erskine's interpretation of identity and salvation, for instance, are at best a reformulation of Christian belief within a Rastafarian framework. For example, the idea of being saved is about conversion to the Christian way of life (Acts 2:37–47; Eph. 2:1–10). Erskine applies this same Christian idea of salvation to Rastafarianism. Nevertheless, it is not clear if the idea of being saved is a Rastafarian concept or a Christian belief that Erskine has imported and applied to Rastafarianism.

Rasta theology teaches that salvation is obtained through knowledge about God. Erskine argues that this is the wrong approach for obtaining salvation. Writing in this regard, he states:

> *Rasta seems to ask...what must I know? This is not the emphasis of Scripture. On the contrary, Scripture directs one to becoming and doing. The central questions are: Who must I become and what must I do to be saved (Mark 10:17; John 3:3).*[44]

This question of being saved is about 'becoming' and 'doing.' But as Erskine points out, Rasta theology needs to make a distinction between knowledge and salvation.[45] What is unclear, however, is the basis and nature of Erskine's critique of the notion of salvation in the theology of Rastafarianism.

Erskine's critique reflects some degree of inconsistency. On one hand, he argues that the emergence of Rastafarianism indicates that salvation can be obtained outside the context of the church. On the other hand, he uses Christian Scripture as the basis for defining salvation. By appealing to the Christian Scripture to provide theological authority and clarity to salvation within the alternative context of liberation that Erskine proposes, suggests the use of Christian framework to define salvation even in non-Christian religion. In this case, while salvation is not limited to the context of church, it is defined by Christianity.

Dianne Stewart follows the same pattern as Erskine. Despite her unsparing critique of Christianity, she is dependent on Christian theological categories to interpret her African-derived religions. For example, she uses the Christian theological categories such as incarnation and the cross[46] in order to advance her claim of the African-derived religions theological system. She is not only using a Christian framework to interpret her claim but also is depending on such a framework to establish the theological legitimacy of African-derived religions.

The strong Christian influences Stewart employs in de-centring the Christian faith as a source of liberation suggests that this theological interpretation of liberation is nothing less than Christianity in non-Christian clothes. It could be argued that Stewart's approach is an attempt to interpret non-Christian religion through Christian lenses. This approach may be considered similar to Robert Beckford's use of the Rastafarian term 'Dread' in his construction of a Black British Theology.[47]

The issue in discussion, however, is not liberation but the context of liberation. Political parties and movements also can claim liberation as their purpose in society.[48] Admittedly, liberation is not limited to Christianity but there is the distinctive element of faith in God as a way of life and basis for liberation which is absent from the shift from the church to non-Christian religions. In this sense, faith in Jesus Christ is not the basis of liberation but in reference to the Sam Sharpe Revolt, faith is central wherein the oppressed discovered the relationship between their struggle for freedom and God's purpose of liberation for humanity.

The Domestication of Black Christianity

Adding to the de-centring of faith, the second issue of liberation without faith is the sinister practice to domesticate Christianity. Theologian Dwight Hopkins calls this practice a form of historical amnesia which ignores the social conditions out of which Black theology emerged.[49] Hopkins speaks for many when he writes: 'This is troublesome because Black theology was never created by an individual sitting in any ivory tower...Black theology arose out of a spiritual and physical life-and-death situation.'[50] Anthony Reddie in his analysis of Black Christianity also recognizes this domestication of Black Christianity. Reddie insightfully describes this trend as '...the folk-oriented approach to Christian traditions that arise out of the black experiences, but which does not have a political or explicitly transformative agenda.'[51]

Representatives of this domesticating trend argue that a theology of liberation is for those who use the dialectic of the poor and oppressed to define themselves.[52] Theology, they argue, while it is contextual, is not defined by the people in their particular context.[53] It is the contention of these religious scholars that liberation from oppression is negative and perpetuates a negative identity[54] and also that Christianity has hegemonic control over Black religion.[55] As one proponent states:

> *The practice of utilizing the slave-master/slave dialectic in the twenty-first century perpetuates the unworthy concept that what Caribbean [Black] people are at their core is rooted in that relationship and that their world-view is defined by it.*[56]

These advocates of domesticated Christianity are primarily addressing the mistaken notion that the search for liberation is about identity. They correctly point out that the experiences of slavery, colonization and oppression do not define the Black person's total identity.[57] Blacks were free people prior to these sad events and tragic experiences in history and are above all, human beings.[58] The rationale for Black liberation, however, is premised on the claim that God has made all persons for freedom. Liberation itself does not create freedom since God has made all persons free and for freedom.[59] Liberation is God's gift to all persons but especially to the poor and the oppressed as the Christian Scripture attests. 'Stand fast therefore in the liberty wherein Christ has set you free…' (Gal. 5:1).

In this regard, the Sam Sharpe Revolt nullifies any attempt to domesticate Black Christianity and demonstrates that Black people are demanding nothing but justice and affirming their rights as free human beings which the following account of protest and resistance against oppression reflects:

> *We have worked enough already…The life we*
> *live is…the life of a dog. We wont be slaves*
> *no more; we wont lift hoe no more; we wont take*
> *flog no more. We free now, we free now; no more slaves again.*[60]

In fact, what the proponents of a domesticated Black Christianity fail to understand is that it is because Black people respect themselves that they seek liberation from oppression and dehumanization. For those who would attempt to domesticate Black Christianity, liberation is not the theological framework nor is the Black experience a normative source for Black theological discourse.[61] The attempt to remove faith in Jesus Christ from the centre of liberation, however, is to de-Christianize Black Christianity in order to advance an inclusive Black religion which may be liberative but not necessarily rooted in faith in Jesus Christ.[62] Anthony Reddie, in his commentary on this pernicious and pervasive trend to domesticate Black Christianity, has observed that the so-called 'prosperity gospel' movement as represented by Black churches [*and leaders* such as Creflo Dollar in the United States and the Kingsway International Christian Centre in Britain are now offering an attractive prosperity-led, non-contextualized approach to Christianity.[63] Reddie also points out that these churches do not use the Black experience as a point of departure in their theology and neither is the Black Church Tradition that defines their theological self-understanding.[64] Notwithstanding this attempt to domesticate Black Christianity, there is a faith tradition which affirms the liberative component of Black Christianity and Black theology as a theology of liberation.

Conclusion

This chapter resists the domestication of Black Christianity and theology which seeks to tame this liberating religion into becoming a religious 'pet' of contemporary society. A domesticated religion reflects a conformist approach in addressing the issue of liberation from oppression and suffering. To promote liberation without faith in Jesus Christ is not only myopic and misleading, but it also blurs and blunts the emancipatory dimension of the gospel of Jesus Christ. The reason this can happen is that it overlooks God's decisive and ongoing liberative involvement in human history. What this trend of liberation without faith then calls for is an alternative perspective of theology with the intent to help us envision reality in a new and different way. This is important in order to bring into existence the life that God has promised and declared in Jesus Christ.

Insisting on liberation through faith, the radical faith of Sam Sharpe is interpreted as an example of the emancipatory dimension of the gospel of Jesus Christ. Thus, the next chapter explores liberation through faith as exemplified through Sam Sharpe's life and execution as an embodiment of faith in Jesus Christ, the liberator of the oppressed.

Notes

1. James Cone, *Liberation: A Black Theology of Liberation* (New York: J.B. Lippincott Co., 1970); see also the very important work of Noel Erskine, *Decolonizing Theology: A Caribbean Perspective* (New York: Orbis Books, 1981). For further exploration see, Kortright Davis, *Emancipation Still Comin': Explorations in Caribbean Theology* (New York: Orbis Books, 1990).
2. Burchell Taylor, 'The Liberated Community as Subversive and Liberating in an Unjust Society,' in *Caribbean Theology: Preparing for*

the Challenges Ahead, ed., Howard Gregory (Kingston: Canoe Press, 1995), 73–78. For a discussion on the prophetic Black Christianity, see J. Deotis Roberts, *The Prophethood of Black Believers: An African American Political Theology for Ministry* (Louisville: Westminster/John Knox Press, 1994); Linda E. Thomas, ed., *Living Stones in the Household of God: The Legacy and Future of Black Theology* (Minneapolis: Fortress Press, 2004); Iva E. Carruthers, Fredrick D. Haynes III and Jeremiah A. Wright, Jr. eds., *Blow the Trumpet in Zion: Global Vision and Action for the 21st Century Black Church* (Minneapolis: Fortress Press, 2005).

3. J. Deotis Roberts, 'A Black Ecclesiology of Involvement,' *Journal of Black Religious Thought* 32 (Spring–Summer 1975): 36, 40; see also James Cone, *Black Theology & Black Power* (New York: Harper & Row, 1969), 91–115.
4. Noel Erskine, *From Garvey to Marley: Rastafari Theology* (Florida: University of Florida Press, 2005), 4.
5. Erskine, 3.
6. Erskine, 114–97.
7. Erskine, 150.
8. Erskine, 152–62.
9. Erskine, 159.
10. Jeremiah Wright, *Africans Who Shaped Our Faith* (Illinois: Urban Ministries Inc., 1995).
11. Kenneth L. Waters, *Afrocentric Sermons: The Beauty of Blackness in the Bible* (Valley Forge: Judson Press, 1993), 73–89.
12. Mark Ellington, *The Riches of Augustine: His Contextual & Pastoral Theology* (Kentucky: Westminster John Knox Press, 2005).
13. Justo L. Gonzalez, *The Story of Christianity: The Early Church to the Dawn of the Reformation*, Vol.1 (Massachusetts Price Press, 1984), 173–80.
14. Thomas C. Oden, *How Africa Shaped the Christian Mind* (Illinois: IVP Books, 2007). This study represents a white conservative evangelical perspective of Christianity. This signifies not only a shift but an open acknowledgement of the African origin of Christianity by a foremost theological tradition in Western Christianity.
15. Randall Bailey, 'The Biblical Basis For a Political Theology of Liberation,' in *Blow the Trumpet in Zion: Global Vision and Action for the 21st Century Black Church*, ed. Iva E. Carruthers, Frederick D. Haynes and Jeremiah A. Wright (Minneapolis: Fortress Press, 2005), 93.
16. Erskine, 1–37.
17. Cited in Robert J. Stewart, *Religion and Society in Post-Emancipation Jamaica* (Knoxville: University of Tennessee Press, 1992), 168.
18. Kelly Brown Douglas, *What's Faith Got to Do With It? Black Bodies/Christian Souls* (New York: Orbis Books, 2005), 71–149.

19. Winston Lawson, *Religion and Race: African and European Roots in Conflict – A Jamaican Testament* (New York; Peter Lang, 1996), 100–226; 240–76.
20. Shirley C. Gordon, *Our Cause for His Glory: Christianisation and Emancipation in Jamaica* (Kingston: University of the West Indies Press, 1998), 121.
21. Jean Besson, *Martha Brae's Two Histories: European Expansion and Caribbean Culture-Building in Jamaica* (Chapel Hill: University of North Carolina Press, 2002; Kingston: Ian Randle Publishers, 2003).
22. Besson, 98. See also Robert Stewart, 110–52.
23. Besson, 98–99.
24. Besson, 100. For a lucid discussion on the relationship between the enslaved and the non-conformist church, see Mary Tuner, *Slave and Missionaries.*
25. Orlando Patterson, *Sociology of Slavery: An Analysis of the Origins, Development, and Structure of Negro Slave Society in Jamaica* (London: Macgibbon & Kee, 1973), 214.
26. Mary Turner, *Slaves and Missionaries: The Disintegration of Jamaican Slave Society, 1787–1834* (Kingston: University of the West Indies Press, 1998), 163–173.
27. Turner, 100; 242.
28. Delroy A. Reid-Salmon, *Home Away From Home The Caribbean Diasporan Church in the Black Atlantic Tradition* (London: Equinox Publishing Company, 2007), 59–74.
29. Diane J. Austin-Broos, *Jamaica Genesis: Religion and the Politics of Moral Order* (Kingston: Ian Randle Publishers, 1997), 178–201.
30. Ibid.
31. Austin-Broos, 240.
32. Dianne M. Stewart, *Three Eyes for the Journey: The African Dimensions of the Jamaica Religious Experience* (New York: Oxford University Press, 2005), 16–187.
33. Dianne Stewart, 199–241.
34. Dianne Stewart, 4.
35. Dianne Stewart, 91–137.
36. Dianne Stewart, 4–6.
37. Ibid.
38. Dianne Stewart, 238.
39. Ibid.
40. Ibid.
41. Dianne Stewart, 68–89.
42. Dianne Stewart, 91–187.
43. Robert Stewart, *Religion and Society in Post-Emancipation Jamaica*

(Knoxville: University of Tennessee Press, 1992), 110–52.
44. Erskine, 196.
45. Ibid.
46. Dianne Stewart, 158–69.
47. Robert Beckford, *Black Theology and Black Culture in Britain* (London: DLT, 1998). See also his, *Dread and Pentecostal: Black Political Theology for the Church in Britain* (London: SPCK, 2000), 160–220.
48. Leslie James, 'Text and the Resistance of Change: Bible and Decolonization in Post-World War II Caribbean Discourse,' in *Religion, Culture and Tradition*, ed. Hemshand Gossai and Samuel Nathaniel Murrell (London: MacMillan Press Ltd., 2000), 143–66.
49. Dwight Hopkins, *Head and Heart: Black Theology-Past, Present and Future* (New York: Palgrave Macmillan, 2002).
50. Hopkins, 162.
51. Reddie, *Black Theology in Transatlantic Dialogue* (New York: Palgrave Macmillan, 2006), 17.
52. J. D. Aldred, *Respect: Understanding Caribbean British Christianity* (Peterborough: Epworth, 2005), 25.
53. Aldred, 24.
54. Victor Anderson, *Beyond Ontological Blackness: An Essay on African American Religious and Cultural Criticism* (New York: Continuum, 1995), 14.
55. Anthony Pinn, *Varieties of African American Religious Experience* (Minneapolis: Fortress Press, 1998).
56. Aldred, 26.
57. Aldred, 24–26.
58. Aldred, 26.
59. Philip Potter and Barbara Wartenberg-Potter, *Freedom is For Freeing* (New York: The United Methodist Church, 1990), 77–80.
60. Cited in Mary Turner, 160.
61. Reddie, 17.
62. Dianne Stewart, *Three Eyes For the Journey: An African Dimension of the Jamaica Religious Experience* (New York: Oxford University Press, 2005); Noel Erskine, *From Garvey to Marley* (Florida: University of Florida Press, 2005); Darnise C. Martin, *Beyond Christianity: African Americans in a New Thought Church* (New York: New York University Press, 2005); Anthony Pinn, *Varieties of African American Religious Experience* (Minneapolis: Fortress Press, 1998).
63. Reddie, 70.
64. Ibid.

5 - Get Up and Stand Up: The Grounds of Liberation

INTRODUCTION

Sam Sharpe gave voice to his faith though his quest for liberation. Sharpe's faith was born out of the contingencies, complexities, struggles and sufferings of Black life. As faith born out of the experience, Sharpe's faith was the product of his quest for the meaning of life. This faith helped him to make sense out of life and carried and sustained him as he encountered the terror of struggle and endured the horror of suffering in the quest for liberation.

Emerging out of this experience are the essential elements of faith within the Black theological tradition that reminded him of the immediate presence of God, his African heritage of a sacred and holistic world that teaches that there is no dichotomy between the sacred reality and material existence, and a God who did not justify slavery or any form of oppression. Throughout this discussion, keep in mind that each aspect of the faith is to be interpreted in light of each other and the liberating purpose of God though Jesus Christ.

The perspective of faith which is proposed is understood not in terms of a body of belief as is embodied in doctrines or in creeds, but as a commitment to a particular way of life that seeks to appropriate and approximate the purpose of God expressed through Jesus Christ. Sam Sharpe both believed and based the pursuit for liberation on his faith in the emancipatory purpose of Jesus Christ whom he used as a source of power and as a theological framework for interpreting the quest for emancipation.

For Sam Sharpe, therefore, faith[1] rooted in Jesus Christ is that dynamic, liberating and transformative power of God that enables the oppressed to navigate life through the turbulent waters of despair and death, pursue human wholeness and affirm the ultimate triumph of God's purpose through Jesus Christ.[2] Faith provides also a theological framework that facilitates the interpretation of human reality.

This interpretation of human reality concerns the issues, questions and challenges that emerge from the experience of the people in seeking a life of dignity. This notion of faith is at the service of Black liberation and helps to determine the priority of Black theology. As such, the meaning of faith in Black theology is not a rational belief or a body of doctrinal statements but a relational act that describes a way of life grounded on the promises of God in Jesus Christ.

This view is advanced in that the issue in discussion is not simply the agent or context but the Christological basis of Black liberation[3] that considers seriously the liberative power of faith to transform the human condition to approximate God's kingdom in history. The emphasis then is on the practice of faith showing how this living by faith relates to social structures and systems. In this regard, the paradigmatic use of the Sam Sharpe Revolt defines faith as equality, freedom, justice and embodiment as the essential features of the faith as the Sam Sharpe Revolt symbolizes.

The Equality of All Persons

The equality of all persons is one of the fundamental elements of the faith of Sam Sharpe. Sharpe unquestionably interpreted his existential condition in light of his faith in Jesus Christ. Writing in this regard the Methodist clergyman Henry Bleby states:

> *He referred to the manifold evils and injustice of slavery, asserted the natural equality of man [human beings] with regard to freedom; and referring to the Holy Scripture as his authority, denied that the white man [person] had any more right to hold blacks in bondage, than blacks had to enslave whites.*[4]

This statement of Sharpe is an eloquent expression of the teaching of the Bible that all persons are equal (Acts 10:34). Euro-American Abolitionists supported this assertion when they premised the basis for the evil and abolition of slavery on this notion of the equality of all human being. In what he termed 'Creation Humanism,' the Baptist historian, John Briggs observes that these abolitionists have argued that:

> *The equality of men [human], as all made by God, was fundamental to Christian doctrine. 'Did we not all spring from one common stock? ...we are all brothers and sisters.'...*

> *This was the importance of the creation story which clearly established that all men [persons] from their Divine creation shared a common nature.*[5]

Briggs' remarks indicate and attest to the claim that Sam Sharpe believed in the equality of all people. Sharpe's view of the human being contended with white supremacy which denies the equality of all people and advocates Black inferiority to people of white pigmentation advancing the view that Blacks are less than human beings. Sharpe, as his Revolt demonstrates, rejected such view as erroneous and evil. The insight of Cornel West sums up this issue.

> *The notion that black people are human beings is a relatively new discovery in the modern West. The idea of black, culture, and intellectual capacity remains problematic and controversial within prestigious halls of learning and sophisticated intellectual circles.*[6]

Racism in West's perspective is ubiquitous and systemic. Sam Sharpe then, as a student of the Bible, was aware of the biblical teaching that all persons are created in the image of God (Gen. 1:26–27). This assertion of the equality of all persons was not only a challenge to the heresy of White superiority but the assertion of a Black Christian theological anthropology. Thus, through the act of revolt, which in itself was an expression of faith, Sharpe demonstrated his philosophy of the human being which was a departure from the dominant philosophy of white superiority and Black inferiority during his time.

Freedom

The second theological principle that defines the faith of Sam Sharpe is freedom. Freedom is a Divine gift of God for humanity through the liberating act of Jesus. He believed that God has not only made all persons equal but also created them for freedom (Gal. 3:26–29). Giving an account of this reason for leading the Revolt, Sharpe expressed the view that by reading the Bible, he came to the conclusion that, 'Whites had no more right to hold the Black people in slavery, than the Black people had to make White people slaves; and, for his own part, he would rather die than live in slavery.'[7] This is a theology grounded in a liberating faith that begins with and is defined by the gospel of Jesus Christ. In support of this perspective, the ecumenical theologians, Philip Potter and Barbel Wartenberg-Potter declare:

> *This theology starts with the gospel of liberation and the call to be servants one of another through love. This theology notes that Jesus our liberator showed a dear solidarity with the poor, the marginalized in the spirit of the prophets.*[8]

On this basis Sharpe is further declaring the meaning of human existence. Freedom is the essence of what it means to be a human being. So, to be free, is to be human. Sharpe is known to have expressed this understanding in his sermons and addresses using biblical texts such as 'No man can serve two masters' (Matt. 6: 24); 'If the Son therefore shall make you free, you shall be free indeed.'(John 8:36); 'Ye are bought with a price: be not ye servants of men' (1 Cor. 7:23).[9]

Here is Sharpe's point of departure from the British abolitionists. The abolitionists premised the claim for the liberation on the atrocities of slavery[10] which they delineated as: 'neglect of instruction, moral and religious to slaves, profanation of Sabbath, barbarity of punishment, licentious treatment of females, discouragement given to marriage, perversion of laws, separation of families by sale, rejection…slave evidence, difficulties in the way of a slave obtaining his freedom and the uncertainty of holding liberty when secured.'[11] But Sharpe, he established the quest for liberation on the Divine right of freedom for all persons. He asserted: 'My brethren, let us be men! If we do not stand up boldly for ourselves and take freedom, then buckra will put us to the muzzles of their guns, and shoot us like pigeons.'[12] As a way of seeking liberation, Sharpe declared on the day of his execution, 23 May 1832, that the reason he was sentenced to death was because he affirmed the right to be free. He expressed as follow: 'I am going to die because I thought I had the right to be free.'[13]

Justice

Justice is the third element of Sam Sharpe's faith. Justice is based on the character of God. It is the act to correct what human beings have done wrong by fulfilling God's liberation for the oppressed and dismantling oppressive systems and structures. Affirming this claim, James Cone writes: 'justice is a part of the Being of God, he [God] is bound to do justly. Whatever God does must be just because he [God] is justice.'[14] In Fred Kennedy's *Daddy Sharpe,* the main protagonist, Sam Sharpe, expresses this view of justice:

> *I know that the Lord will change our condition because he [God] is just. I have told my fellow slaves to be of good courage for He [God] will strengthen their hearts, all those who hope in the Lord. I teach them Psalm 34 which tells us that blessed is the man [human being] who trusteth in the Lord. None shall be desolate who trust in him [God].*[15]

In light of this remark, Sharpe must have learned from his reading of the Biblical Witness and from the teachings of his African heritage that justice is an expression of faith.[16] Insisting on the rightness of the cause of liberation, Sharpe explained that, 'he thought and learnt from his Bible, that the whites had no more right to hold black people in slavery, than black people had to make white people slave; and for his own part, he would rather die than to live in slavery.'[17] This suggests that he believed that oppression is against God's will. Clarence S. Reid makes this claim powerfully in his *Samuel Sharpe: From Slavery To National Hero:* 'Sharpe himself had great respect for the Word, and claimed that it was from his reading of Scriptures that he came to the conclusion that all men [*human being*]had a right to be free.'[18]

In this sense, Peter Paris argues that justice is the supreme virtue because it seeks the good of both individuals and the community. Paris writes: 'the ultimate goal of justice is also the preservation and promotion of community...Such thought is fundamentally different from Western Enlightenment political philosophies, which are primarily interested in protecting individual rights and property.'[19] Departing from a Euro-American perspective of justice, Paris is pointing out that justice in Black theology is communal and individualistic. This form of reasoning deepened Sharpe's commitment and underscored his willingness to pay the ultimate price for obtaining justice. Expressing the depth of this commitment, Sharpe stated, 'the law by which he died has been broken, pronounced that law itself is treason against God.'[20]

Justice for Sharpe also means liberation from oppression. Slavery was an evil and unjust system. As Clarence S. Reid observes: 'The indignities, the abuses and manifold cruelties which were daily perpetrated among and upon them, the way in which the scales – not only of society but of justice such as it was – were totally weighed against them, were too obvious and immediate. Injustice was their life.'[21] Sharpe was neither content nor willing to remain in this state of life. It was on this basis he established the rightness of the cause to rebel against slavery. Sharpe made this clear at the first planning meeting for the Revolt at the house of one of his colleagues, Colonel Johnson. During this meeting, Sharpe thoroughly reviewed the nature of slavery, the debate surrounding it and the implications for them.[22] Writing regarding this meeting, Henry Bleby, the Methodist clergyman, who interviewed Sharpe while he was in prison, reported that 'he referred to the manifold evils and injustice of slavery.'[23] According to Reid, 'All Sharpe needed to point out was that slavery was not a natural state, and it did not have to exist. It was unjust.'[24] As such, justice is the application of the will of God to the social system, structure and conditions of society. Kennedy describes the state in this way:

> *I ask you, for a moment, to reflect how it must feel to be the chattel of someone else, to be bought and sold in the marketplace, to be driven like oxen to the field to labor all day, to be beaten by the master so that you will work harder, and to be fed along with the other animals, not when you are hungry but when it is decided that it is feed time. You are fed not for the enjoyment of food or the satisfaction of hunger but so that the master may keep you strong and fit for his own economic gain.*[25]

This insightful portrayal of Sharpe's reaction to enslavement underscores the belief that, 'justice is the divine decision to vindication of the poor, the needy and the helpless.'[26] Put differently, justice is the vindication of the poor, oppressed and those who the society marginalizes and does not protect under the law. These are the people who are not only unprotected but are dehumanized, degraded and exploited by the law. Kennedy explains the nature of this desire in another portrayal of Sharpe's description of slavery:

> *The beasts of the earth, the asses, the cows, the pigs do not*

receive the harshness of treatment that we do. Even though we are all the property of the landowner, the animals in the pen are treated with more respect. Their heads are not cut from their bodies and hang upon poles. They are not flogged until they bleed. Buckets of salt are not thrown on their open wounds. They are not bound in chains and placed in stocks.[27]

Thinking further about justice as an element of Sharpe's faith, the contradictions between faith in God and slavery convinced him that it is just to seek liberation from slavery.[28] The appropriate human response to any injustice is to make right that which is wrong in the society based on God's character and purpose. Otherwise put, to be human means to affirm God's justice which may require going against the law of the country. In his conversation with Bleby, Sharpe asserted that he was not wrong to seek liberation and if he were wrong, his faith in God assured him of forgiveness. Sharpe stated: 'If I have done wrong in that, I trust I shall be forgiven; for I cast myself upon the Atonement…I depend for salvation upon the Redeemer, who shed his blood upon Calvary for sinners.'[29]

Concurring with Sharpe's claim of the inherent contraction and inconsistency between the Christian Faith and slavery, the British Baptist missionary pastor, William Knibb gave the following testimony to the British Parliament:

British Parliament: Do you believe it to be possible for Religion and Slavery to exist together for any length of time?

Knibb: I think not.

British Parliament: You do not think any very considerable progress can be made in religious knowledge during the existence of Slavery?

Knibb: My opinion of Christianity is that it will induce in the mind of every possessor a love for freedom ... [but] Christianity and slavery are incompatible.[30]

Here, Sam Sharpe did not compromise his faith. Instead, his faith compelled him to seek justice in the hope of obtaining liberation. In this struggle, justice emerges as a 'response to God's call to be obedient'[31] to the Divine purpose of liberation. Summing up the justification to rebel against oppression, Sharpe made it clear to his colleagues that: 'If buckra would pay them, they would work as before; but if any attempt was made to force them as slaves, they would fight for their freedom.'[32] What this suggests is that liberation is not without a cost; it encompasses a faith that embodies the vision of life and human society in order to give birth to the new heaven and earth promised in Jesus Christ.

> *Here is my servant, whom I have chosen, the one I love, in whom I delight; I will put my Spirit on him, and he will proclaim justice to the nations. He will not quarrel or cry out; no one will hear his voice in the streets. A bruised reed he will not break, and a smoldering wick he will not snuff out, till he leads justice to victory. In his name the nations will put their hope* (Isaiah 42:1–4; Matt. 12:18–21).

This is the reality faith envisions. Faith envisions a world that transcended the social conditions and experience, enables one to grasp the rightness of the cause for liberation despite fierce contradictions and persistent conflicts. Sharpe, for example, believed, nevertheless, that when you have faith in God by seeking equality, freedom and justice, you cannot fail. The victory is not the outcome of the struggle but the rightness of the cause.

Embodiment

Faith in Jesus Christ is the basis for liberation from oppression. In advancing this idea previously, in chapter four, attention is called to the notion of liberation without faith by exploring the trend to eliminate faith from the centre of the human pursuit for liberation and the attempt to domesticate Black Christianity and indirectly, Black theology. In this chapter so far, the core elements of this faith have been examined. Next to be examined is one additional aspect of faith worth considering. This examination is necessary to illustrate how faith inspires liberation and to identify a resource for countering misunderstanding about the theological basis of the Black struggle for liberation and the fullness of life. In so doing, it will be shown that along with equality, freedom and justice, paying the price through embodiment is an essential component of faith.

In promoting this notion, it is contended that the faith of Sam Sharpe which he ultimately expressed through his execution represents identification with Christ's own passion and commitment to human liberation and serves as a model of a liberating faith. Indeed, Sam Sharpe's experience of suffering and death has established a Black tradition of embodied faith based on the emancipatory purpose of Jesus Christ. This symbolic representation of faith is indicated in the following remarks that he made: 'I have rebelled against the laws of the country and am now about to make a sacrifice of my life as an atonement.' [33]

By this statement, Sharpe was not suggesting that he was going to die for the liberation of oppressed humanity. Put differently, Sharpe was not paying with his life the price for sin as Jesus did according to Christian theology.[34] Rather, Sharpe's statement is a testimony of his faith emphasizing the conviction that suffering, even paying with one's life, is an inherent factor in the struggle for liberation. It is further insisted that Sam Sharpe as leader of the oppressed through his execution was the one through whom the oppressed community found a visible expression of liberation. In identification with Christ this community has emerged as a newly constituted liberated people of God.

The attitude of Sharpe and his fellow Freedom Fighters towards their execution illustrate their absolute commitment to the Christian Faith as evidence of being God's people. They gave their lives in confidence, dignity and courage in a manner similar to the prophetic description of the crucified Christ that the biblical testimony affirms: 'He was oppressed and afflicted, yet he did not open his mouth; he was like a lamb to the slaughter, and as a sheep before her shearers is silent... By oppression and judgment he was taken away' (Isaiah 53:7–8ff). Understanding the Freedom Fighters of the Sam Sharpe Revolt in light of this biblical statement, the historical record states: They were 'calm and undismayed...as if they had been proceeding to their daily toil... with dignified bearing of men untroubled as to the justice of their cause they yielded themselves to their doom.'[35] As for Sam Sharpe, Winston Lawson describes him as reflecting 'moral courage and commitment to the cause of liberty.'[36] Henry Bleby's testimonial of Sam Sharpe attests to Lawson's claim. For Bleby, Sharpe was 'such a man...as was likely, nay, certain had he been set free to commence another struggle for freedom, and it was certain, the slaves would have joined him.'[37]

The following account of the execution of Sam Sharpe's supporters clearly and dramatically demonstrates the idea of embodying the liberative dimension of the gospel of Jesus Christ:

> *The gibber erected in the public square in the centre of the town was seldom without occupants during the day, for many weeks, generally four, seldom less than three, were hung at once. The bodies remained stiffening in the breeze, till the court martial had provided another batch of victims... [The Executioner] would ascend a ladder and with his knife sever the ropes by which the poor creatures were suspended and let them fall to the ground.*
>
> *Other victims would then be...suspended in their places and cut down in their turn...the whole heap of bodies remaining just as they fell until the work-house negroes came in the evening with carts and took them away, to be cast into a pit for the purpose, a little distance out of town.*[38]

Fully convinced of the righteousness of the Revolt against slavery and expressing his commitment to die for this cause, Sam Sharpe proudly acknowledged breaking the law of the land when he said; 'I have rebelled against the laws of the country and am now about to make a sacrifice of my life as an atonement.'[39] When asked if he had any regrets for his action, Sharpe said, after much thought: 'I am sorry that so many people have died as a result of my actions. I am also sorry that so much property has been destroyed. But I have done nothing wrong in demanding my freedom. For this I will not apologize.'[40] He went as far as to define his actions as an expression of his call to be a Christian as the following statement indicates. 'Let me beg you my brethren, to attend to your Christian duties for it is the only way for you to go to salvation.'[41]

If anyone should be in doubt about his conviction of the righteousness of his action and commitment to liberation, such person should consider Sharpe's final remarks on the day of his execution. 'I would rather die on yonder gallows than live in slavery.'[42] Sam Sharpe's convictions and actions in this regard were an echo of the beliefs of his comrades in oppression. They said: 'We have worked enough already. The life we live is...the life of a dog. We won't be slaves no more; we wont lift hoe no more; we wont take flog no more. We are free now; no more slaves.'[43]

These accounts might be seen in terms of identification with the cruel and agonizing suffering of Jesus on the cross that wicked men and women meted out to him (Acts 2:23; 4:27–28). Just as Jesus died a death of shame and suffering so too these Freedom Fighters met an undignified death. Their testimony and experience indicate to me how they interpreted the reality of having faith in Jesus Christ in terms of the Scripture which states: 'If anyone will come after me, let him [*her*] deny himself [*herself*], take up his [*her*]cross and follow me daily' (Matt. 16:24). This principle is expressed also in the following manner. 'We must through much tribulation enter the kingdom of God' (Acts 14:22). While on one hand, it is believable that the cross is the revelation of God's love for humanity which James Cone so eloquently states, 'Today, yesterday, the cross reveals God's solidarity with the unspeakable suffering of those who were tortured and put to death by human cruelty.'[44] Yet on the other hand, I still maintain that Black suffering can be regarded as an embodiment of the emancipatory dimension of God's gospel of liberation.

Sam Sharpe is not the only person who embodied the emancipatory dimension of the gospel. This manner of embodying the gospel can be considered to be normative in the Black liberation struggle for freedom. Attention should be called to a number of Freedom Fighters and liberators who fall into this category. The African, Harriet Tubman (1823–1913), also known as 'Moses,' for example, among many others, risked her life for the liberation of her people during the time of slavery. She was involved in the anti-slavery movement in North America but is especially known for leading more than 300 enslaved persons over a period of seven years (1850–57) into freedom through the Underground Railroad Movement.[45]

Ida B. Wells is another example par excellence of one who has embodied the emancipatory aspect of the gospel of liberation. She represents leadership of the Anti-lynching Campaign during the 1880s and through her writings as a journalist inspired the Black community to defend themselves against White violence. In an editorial in the newspaper, *Free Speech,* she wrote: 'The city of Memphis has demonstrated that neither character nor standing avails the Negro if he [*she*] dares to protect himself [*herself]* against the white man [*person*] or become his [*her*] rival.'[46] Putting this statement into practice, Wells purchased a gun and suggested that others follow her example fully convinced and prepared to 'sell her life as dearly as possible.'[47] In order not to misconstrue Wells's admonition, readers should note that she was not advocating violence against her opponents. She was rather expressing the need for personal responsibility of defending oneself against injustice.

Martin Luther King, Jr is included also in this tradition of embodying the gospel through one's lifestyle. He stated that:

> *...if physical death is the price that a man [one] must pay to free his [one's] children and his [one's] white brethren from permanent death of the spirit, then nothing could be more redemptive. This is the type of soul force that I am convinced will triumph over the physical force of the oppressor.*[48]

This is not an isolated remark by King. It is rather a remark that expresses one of his convictions about the morality and righteousness of his cause. King is reported to have expressed this conviction when he said: 'I feel though that my cause is so right, so moral, that if I should lose my life, in some way it would aid the cause.'[49]

The Former South Africa President, Nelson Mandela, epitomizes also the embodiment of the emancipatory dimension of God's liberating purpose for humanity. In his 1964 defence speech, 'I am the First Accused,' at his own trial for leading the liberation struggle against apartheid in South Africa said:

> *During my lifetime I have dedicated myself to this struggle of the African people. I have fought against white domination. I have fought against black domination. I have cherished the ideal of a democratic and free society in which all persons live together in harmony and with equal opportunities. It is an ideal which I hope to live for and to achieve. But if needs be, it is an ideal for which I am prepared to die.*[50]

Mandela was imprisoned for 27 years (1964–90) for seeking liberation from the oppressive, wicked and evil system of apartheid.

Concurring with the claim that Black suffering is a way of embodying a dimension of the gospel of Jesus Christ and at the same time, writing of the cost that Caribbean Diasporan people pay in their experience of seeking to obtain a better life in countries other than their own, Anthony Reddie notes: 'Throughout the years, black people have felt the call to pay the price and to follow through until the very end, no matter what they might experience or meet along the way.'[51]

There are different ways of embodying the emancipatory aspect of the gospel because not all persons are able to embody this gospel in the same manner as Sam Sharpe, the above mentioned persons and others not mentioned. In support of this view, Reddie has noted that: 'millions of black people have decided that it is better to take the harder option and ignore the easier alternative, in order that they might achieve what they felt they needed to do.'[52]

This Black theology is the way of life grounded in faith and life pattern of Jesus where Black identity and experience are the heuristic for interpreting God's emancipatory purpose. It incorporates understanding salvation as liberation from sin and oppression, the empowerment of the weak and powerless, the formation of communities of faith and a transformation of society.[53] Anthony Reddie has assigned authoritative voice to this definition of Black theology when he writes:

> *When speaking of black theology, I am referring to the specific self-named discipline of reinterpreting Christian traditions and practices in light of liberation themes and concepts, which arise out of the black experience...In effect Blackness becomes the primary interpretive framework for interpreting and reimaging God and the Christian faith.*[54]

Thus, faith sees the distorted relationship between God's purpose and the human condition. Faith sees oppression, exploitation, suffering and then reads this reality differently by motivating the oppressed to take action against such contradictory conditions. In this way, faith sees the way ahead, the way God wants us to go and considers the reality of the way in light of God's purpose and plan which are undefeatable. This suggests that faith yearns for liberty, for 'where the Spirit of Christ is, there is liberty' (2 Cor. 3:17) and thus compels oppressed people to seek liberation in this world and not the world to come.

Conclusion

The fundamental claim of faith as central to liberation has been affirmed by the Sam Sharpe Revolt. Even though there is a force to marginalize faith, it cannot be eliminated from the life of the oppressed. The role of faith in the life of the oppressed, that Sam Sharpe represents, has been made clear in their quest for liberation. The concern for liberation has either been de-emphasized or incorporated into the status-quo by theologies that have become content with the current state of human affairs. Theology, therefore cannot afford to dismiss faith.

As seen in the case of Sam Sharpe, the faith of the oppressed is a premise for liberation. We may want to have liberation without faith but Sam Sharpe represents an alternative path that links and relates faith in Jesus Christ to the social structures and existence. In this case, a theology of the Black struggle for liberation is defined from the point a view of those who have faith in God.

Ultimately, the oppressed embody the faith. This embodiment can take the form of suffering. It demonstrates that such embodiment is inevitable for realizing God's purpose in history. This assertion indicates that the embodiment of the emancipatory dimension of the gospel by the oppressed encapsulates their resistance to oppression.

Considering the human condition in light of the Christian Faith, theology becomes emancipatory because it is rooted in confidence in the gospel of Jesus Christ as a means of interpreting the concrete and existential conditions of life. At the same time no exclusive claim to liberation is made but rather an expression that the Christian Faith has its own resources to fulfill God's purpose for humanity. As such, this Faith does not require nor need any external factors for validation. In his noteworthy book, *God of the Oppressed,* theologian James Cone describes the sufficiency of the Christian Faith:

> *Christian theologians must admit that their logic is not the same as other form of rational discourse. The coming of God in Jesus Christ breaks open and thereby creates an experience of truth-encounter that makes us talk in ways often not understandable to those who have not had the experience.*[55]

Sam Sharpe demonstrated both the sufficiency of the Christian Faith as well as a theology that is intrinsically liberative. In this regard, Black theology should not be regarded as whimsical, passive or tame, but rather as radical, prophetic, emancipatory and as a corrective to the notion of liberation without faith.

While other social agencies can carry out the work of liberation, faith defines and underscores the specific nature of God's emancipatory act of solidarity with the oppressed and offers a new life to all. Put differently, since faith is born out of the struggle for liberation, the oppressed has a right to take their freedom. The theological basis for this undertaking is discussed next.

Notes

1. C. S. Reid, *Samuel Sharpe: From Slave to National Hero* (Kingston: Bustamante Institute of Public and International Affairs, 1998), 62. See also, Mary Turner, *Slaves and Missionaries: The Disintegration of Jamaican Slave Society, 1787–1834* (Kingston: University of the West Indies Press, 1998), 132–78.
2. Neville Callam, 'Hope: A Caribbean Perspective,' *Ecumenical Review* 50 (1998): 137–42.
3. James Cone, *God of the Oppressed* (San Francesco: Harper & Row, 1975), 108– 37.
4. Henry Bleby, *Death Struggles of Slavery* (London: Hamilton, Adams and Co., 1835), 114.
5. John H. Y. Briggs, 'Baptist and the Campaign to Abolish the Slave Trade,' *Baptist Quarterly* Vol. 42, October (2007): 270–71.
6. Cornel West, *Prophesy Deliverance: An Afro-American Revolutionary Christianity* (Philadelphia: Westminster Press, 1982), 47. For a stimulating discussion on the origin and construction of racism, see Mervyn C. Alleyne, *The Construction and Representation of Race and Ethnicity in the Caribbean and the World* (Kingston: University of the West Indies Press, 2002).
7. Henry Bleby, cited in Winston Arthur Lawson, *Religion And Race: African and European Roots in Conflict – A Jamaican Testament* (New York: Peter Lang, 1996), 169.
8. Philip Potter and Barbel Wartenberg-Potter, *Freedom is for Freeing*, (New York: United Methodist Church, 1990), 79–80.
9. Cited in C. S. Reid, *Samuel Sharpe: From Slave to National Hero* (Kingston: Bustamante Institute of Public and International Affairs, 1988), 60.

10. Devon Dick, *The Cross and the Machete: Native Baptists of Jamaica – Identity, Ministry and Legacy* (Kingston: Ian Randle Publishers, 2010), 160.
11. John Clarke, *Memorials of Baptist Missionaries in Jamaica, Including the Sketch of Labours of the Early Religious* (London: Yates and Alexander, 1869), 109–10.
12. Henry Bleby, *Scenes in the Caribbean Sea: Being Sketches from a Missionary's Notebook* (London: 1854), 17, 19.
13. Clarke, 107.
14. James H. Cone, *Black Theology & Black Power* (New York: Harper & Row, 1969), 44.
15. Fred W. Kennedy, *Daddy Sharpe: A Narrative of the Life and Adventures Of Samuel Sharpe, A West Indian Slave Narrative Written by Himsself, 1832* (Kingston: Ian Randle Publishers, 2008), 134.
16. Bleby, 111,116.
17. Henry Bleby, *Death Struggles of Slavery* (London: Hamilton, Adams and Co., 1858), 116.
18. C.S. Reid, *Samuel Sharpe: From Slave To National Hero,* (Kingston: Bustamante Institute of Public Affairs, 1988), 60.
19. Peter Paris, *The Spirituality of African Peoples: The Search for a Common Moral Discourse* (Minneapolis: Fortress Press, 1995), 152.
20. Clarke, 161.
21. Reid, 59.
22. Reid, 60.
23. Bleby, 111.
24. Reid, 59.
25. Kennedy, 133–34.
26. Cone, (1969), 43.
27. Kennedy, 134.
28. Bleby, 116.
29. Samuel Sharpe, recorded in Henry Bleby, 117–18.
30. British Parliament Papers, (London: British Museum, 1832), 736.
31. James H. Cone, (1975), 207.
32. Bleby, 112.
33. Sam Sharpe, cited in Reid, 92.
34. Gustaf Aulen, Christus Victor: *An Historical Study of the Three Main Types of Idea of the Atonement, Trans. A. G. Herbert* (New York: Macmillan, 1969. For a study on the atonement in Black theology, see JoAnne Marie Terrell, *Power in the Blood: The Cross in the African American Experience* (New York: Orbis Books, 1998). See also, James A. Noel and Matthew V. Johnson, eds., *The Passion of the Lord: African American*

Reflections (Minneapolis: Fortress Press, 2005).

35. Cited in Mary Turner, 162.
36. Lawson, 159.
37. Cited in Mary Turner, 162.
38. Ibid.
39. Sam Sharpe, cited in Reid, 92.
40. Sam Sharpe, cited in Catherine House, *Voices Against Slavery: Ten Christians Who Spoke out for Feedom* (Scotland: Christian Focus Publications Ltd., 2006), 84.
41. Sam Sharpe, cited in Reid, 93.
42. Bleby, cited in Lawson, 159.
43. Cited Turner, 160.
44. Cone, 52.
45. C. Eric Lincoln and Lawrence H. Mamiya, *The Black Church in the African American Experience* (Durham: Duke University Press, 1990), 282.
46. Cited in Paula Giddings, *When and Where I Enter: The Impact of Black Women on Race and Sex in America* (New York: Bantam Books, 1985), 19.
47. Cited in Giddings, 20.
48. Martin Luther King, Jr. cited in *A Testament of Hope: The Essential Writings and Speeches of Martin Luther King, Jr.* ed., James M. Washington (San Francisco: Harper Collins, 1991), 149.
49. King, *Testament of Hope,* 356. For an illuminating discussion on this subject, see James H. Cone, *Martin & Malcolm & America: A Dream or A Nightmare* (New York: Orbis Books, 1991), 213–43.
50. Nelson Mandela, quoted in Anthony Sampson, *Mandela: The Authorized Biography,* Anthony Sampson (New York: Alfred A. Knopf, 1999), 192. For a personal account of Nelson Mandela's quest for freedom, see *Long Walk to Freedom,* Nelson Mandela (1994).
51. Anthony Reddie, *Growing into Hope: Liberation and Change* (Peterborough: Methodist Publishing House, 1998), 60.
52. Ibid.
53. James H. Cone, (1969); See also Noel Leo Erskine, *Decolonizing Theology: A Caribbean Perspective* (New York: Orbis Books, 1981); Kortright Davis, *Emancipation Still Comin': Explorations in Caribbean Emancipatory Theology* (New York: Orbis Books, 1990); Deloris Williams, *Sisters in the Wilderness: The Challenge of Womanist God-Talk* (New York: Orbis Books, 1993);* James H. Harris, *Preaching Liberation* (Minneapolis: Fortress Press, 1995).
54. Reddie, (2006), 17.
55. James Cone, (1975), 191.

6 - Uprising: The Power of the Oppressed

INTRODUCTION

Undoubtedly, the Sam Sharpe Revolt made an enormous impact on society. From a Black theological perspective, it is, however, indisputable that this Revolt played a major role in the abolition of slavery. The scholarly consensus is that the Revolt set in motion a series of events that ultimately led to the demise of the institution of slavery. Henry Bleby grasped this notion that the Revolt was a lethal weapon of the enslaved in their struggle against oppression. Bleby offered an honest appraisal of the Revolt. He acknowledged its limitation and then concluded with his observation of powerful consequences of the Revolt. Bleby states:

> *The revolt failed to accomplish the immediate purpose of its authors; yet by it, a further wound was dealt to slavery which accelerated its destruction, for it demonstrated to the imperial legislature that among the Negroes themselves, the spirit of freedom had been so widely diffused as to render it most perilous to postpone the settlement of the most important question of emancipation to a later period.*[1]

Richard Hart in his important book, *Slaves Who Abolished Slavery: Blacks in Rebellion*, concurs with this honest acknowledgement of the significant impact the Sam Sharpe Revolt had on Western slaveholding society. Hart summarizes concisely this notion of the abolition of slavery, 'The *[Freedom Fighters]* succeeded in making slavery an insupportably expensive system to maintain.'[2]

Indeed, it cannot be denied, ignored or dismissed that the Sam Sharpe Revolt initiated decisive political, social and theological changes that transformed at least the societies of Britain and the former colonies known today as the Commonwealth Caribbean.[3] For instance, immediately following the Sam Sharpe Revolt, after years of enslaved resistances and the British Abolitionist campaigns that were discussed in chapter two, efforts were intensified to terminate the practice of slavery which included the active engagement of the non-conformist churches, particularly through the work of the British Baptist missionary pastors, William Knibb[4] and Thomas Burchell.[5] Also, the Slave Trade Act which outlawed the trading of human beings became law one year (1833) after the Sam Sharpe Revolt, followed by the abolition of slavery throughout the British colonies in 1834.

Writing of the global impact of this Revolt, C. S. Reid, in his resourceful book, *Samuel Sharpe: From Slave to National Hero*, states: 'Sam Sharpe struck the hammer-blow against an economic and social system which was entrenched in the Americas, and which many considered essential to the *continued prosperity of Europe*'[6] In light of these epoch making events and the timing of their realization, it is arguable that the Sam Sharpe Revolt paved the way for the abolition of slavery and contributed to creating a just and free society.

Given this perspective of the Sam Sharpe Revolt, the Biblical Witness with its definitive message of liberation is employed as the theological basis of the Sam Sharpe Revolt. In making this claim, the chapter includes a definition of the term Biblical Witness and a discussion of the testimonies of three witnesses; namely, the Exodus Story, Prophetic Tradition and the Gospel of Jesus Christ.

Biblical Witness: A Definition

The Biblical Witness consists of the Exodus Story,[7] the Prophetic Tradition and the Gospel of Jesus Christ. Biblical Witness does not mean reading the Bible and then applying the interpretation that is deduced from such reading to the immediate context or the situation. The Biblical Witness, certainly, is not justification of an act or event or a form of proof text. Instead, the Biblical Witness is the account of God's involvement in human history for liberation and freedom. This account concerns the dialogical engagement between the Biblical Witness and the social context. In this engagement, the Biblical Witness identifies with the Black experience and at the same time, the Black experience becomes the lens through which we can interpret the meaning of God's revelation in history.[8]

Pertaining to the Sam Sharpe Revolt, the Biblical Witness provides the basis for interpreting this act as a theological response to injustice, acceptance of the promise of new social order and living in anticipation of the eschatological vision of a different world to symbolize freedom and hope. Armed with this definition of the Biblical Witness, we now begin to examine the testimony of the witnesses beginning with the Exodus Story.

The Exodus Story

The Exodus Story is one of the three Biblical Witnesses that constitute the theological framework for interpreting the meaning of the Sam Sharpe Revolt. The Exodus Story is the paradigm par excellence of the liberator God. The story testifies of God's involvement in history as the liberator who dismantles the system of oppression, demands justice and liberates the oppressed. The entire account of the Exodus Story attests to God as liberator based on the revelation of God to Moses, 'I have seen the misery…'(Exod. 3:7–8), the song of Miriam celebrating God's victory over the oppressor (Exod. 15:1–21) 'Sing to the Lord, for he is highly exalted. The horse and its rider hath he thrown into the sea' (Exod. 15:21) and Moses' farewell address which summarized the journey of the people towards freedom and hope (Deut. 32:1–47).

The contents of the Exodus Story reveal the nature and will of God, constitute the basis of the enslaved's understanding of God as liberator and serve as a resource for one to have confidence in God. This God, for the enslaved, takes side with the oppressed and destroys systems of oppression. This was precisely how God acted through the Sam Sharpe Revolt suggesting that persons, systems and powers that claim human beings as their property are an illusion and any system that is able to practise injustice is anti-God and is on the path to defeat and destruction. From the outset of this quest for liberation, the clear distinction and purposeful intent of the religion of the enslaved is established. For just as the Exodus Story tells of God liberating a specific people, the Hebrews, from slavery, the enslaved, through the Sam Sharpe Revolt recognized their own aspirations for liberation. The message of the Exodus Story signified God's will that they, too, should be liberated.

As this involvement of God is detected in the concrete issues of the life of the enslaved, Black theology employs the Exodus Story as a framework for understanding God's active involvement in human affairs. Liberation theologians such as James Cone, employ the Exodus Story as a paradigm to interpret what God is doing in history. Cone advocates the view that the Biblical Witness as seen in the Exodus Story demonstrates the liberation of the oppressed and that God is on their side. Cone makes this clear in his outstanding text, *God of the Oppressed.*

> *The Exodus was the decisive event in Israel's history, because through it Yahweh revealed himself as the Savior of an oppressed people...In the Exodus event, God is revealed by means of his acts on behalf of a weak and defenseless people. He is the God of power and of strength, able to destroy the enslaving power of mighty Pharaoh.*[9]

For Cone, the Exodus Story attests to a God who liberates. He directs us to the task of asking what the Biblical Witness has to say about social conditions but not to ask what the social context has to say to the Biblical Witness. Cone undoubtedly is aware of the ideological issues to be explored both in the biblical story and in the social context. He, nevertheless, is careful to note that 'the God of the Bible is involved in history...liberating the weak and the helpless from pain and humiliation.'[10]

Significant as the Exodus Story is to interpreting the Sam Sharpe Revolt, there are drawbacks. The story is not an adequate representation of the Black experience. Allen Callahan puts the issue most pointedly. Writing about the meaning of the Exodus Story in the Black experience, he addresses the ambiguity of the story: 'Some African Americans [*Blacks*] have found the account of the suffering of the Hebrew inadequate to the task of expressing the barbarity of American slavery and its aftermath.'[11] Taking Callahan's insights into account, the limitations of the Exodus Story do not nullify the claim that liberation is its central message. It is the message of the Exodus Story and not the story itself which constitutes the framework for the theological interpretation of the Sam Sharpe Revolt.

Black religious scholars, however, including Robert Beckford, have pointed out that the Exodus Story should not be employed uncritically because such usage could lead to the idea of a God who justified the Israelites killing the inhabitants of Canaan to take possession of their country. Beckford acknowledges the merit of this paradigm, but argues that the paradigm advances the view of God as both liberator and oppressor. This suggests that reconciliation becomes the goal of liberation. As Beckford states: 'Therefore, the act of liberation itself must ultimately result in the embracing of the Other who has been your oppressor. This is the ultimate goal of the One who dies at Calvary.'[12]

Who is this Other of whom Beckford speaks? He seems to have borrowed the term from Miroslav Volf, who in his book, *Exclusion & Embrace,* uses the term Other to symbolize the perpetrators of evil and as the enemy.[13] The term Other, therefore, according to Beckford's usage, is certainly not referring to the oppressed but rather to the oppressor. If this is the case, then under what conditions should reconciliation take place? Beckford may have forgotten that the field for facilitating reconciliation is not level or equal. If reconciliation must take place with the Other, the oppressor as he argues, then the conditions that created the breach and separation and the system that sustained it must first be eliminated. More importantly, in order for there to be reconciliation between the oppressed and the oppressor, it calls for a redistribution of power and resources so that all persons will have equal access and opportunity to the resources of society so that they can realize their full potential and experience the fullness of life.[14]

Here, it is insisted that reconciliation with the Other means a theological and ethical commitment to liberation. What Beckford may have overlooked in his claim for reconciliation as the goal of liberation is that unless the Other enters into solidarity with the oppressed, there cannot be any reconciliation. The Other participates in and benefits from the system of oppression. For example, society is usually structured and orientated in ways that carry enormous social advantages in areas such as housing, employment, education, health care and many other issues.[15] Those enjoying the privileges of this intersection of the race, class and gender are the centre of structural power and those without such power are relegated to the margins of society. Justice demands that we ask, examine and reorder society so that all persons can participate and enjoy life. As Catholic ethicist, Barbara Hilert Andolsen asks, 'Do social institutions function to marginalize certain groups while maintaining a pattern of excessive social privileges for another group or groups?'[16] Andolsen asserts that, 'The concept of social justice prods us to ask such *question* [s] about society's treatment of persons and about fairness of the outcomes produced by interlocking social institutions.'[17] Andolsen's assertion is in recognition of the fact that the Other usually make decisions and structure society according to his values and beliefs. Consequently, he is unable to change the system which has blinded his eyes to his own oppression.[18]

But then, the Exodus Story is not about reconciliation with oppressors. The Story is about God liberating oppressed people as is the case of the Sam Sharpe Revolt. The Exodus Story, nevertheless, is not the only biblical account which can be used to interpret the theological meaning of the Sam Sharpe Revolt.

The Prophetic Tradition

The Prophetic Tradition is also a framework for interpreting the Sam Sharpe Revolt. Liberation of the oppressed, as in the case of the Exodus Story, is the central message of the Prophetic Tradition.[19] The Prophetic Tradition is that radical engagement of proclaiming and critiquing society in light of God's purpose of liberation for humanity.[20] The tradition affirms that God willed liberation, justice and freedom for all persons and thereby calls and points human beings and society to respond and endeavour to make these truths become reality in history.[21]

Although the prophets prophesied in different times, each was entrusted with God's message of liberation for the oppressed whose destiny was at stake. Each prophet declared God as the liberator of the oppressed who is involved in human affairs. The biblical prophet Jeremiah, prophesying against Israel's oppression of the people, declares: 'But your eyes and heart are only on your dishonest gain, for shedding innocent blood, and for practicing oppression and violence' (Jer. 22:17). Armed with this understanding of God's will of liberation for the oppressed, the message of the prophet Micah encapsulates this tradition. He asks rhetorically: '...and what does the Lord require of you? To act justly and to love mercy and to walk humbly with your God?' (Micah 6:8). The prophet is making it plain that in a world where evil, corruption and injustice seem to dominate the order of life, the Almighty God demands that all persons be engaged in the struggle for justice and freedom. Amos, joining the chorus of prophetic voices,[22] declares: 'But let justice roll on like a river, righteousness like a never-failing stream' (Amos 5:25).

The message of these prophets affirms the liberating purpose of God. So, as the prophets called attention to God's presence in the midst of human affairs, confronted, critiqued and challenged the social order and espoused God's will for humanity – especially for the poor and oppressed – so did the Sam Sharpe Revolt. The British Baptist missionary, John May, attests to this interpretation of the Sam Sharpe Revolt. May writes:

The Spirit of Freedom moves forth o'er the deep,
And the elements wake from the silence of sleep;
True, the strife may be fierce but the Herald of Light
Speaks of beauty, and Order, and Quiet, and Right,
Move on, blessed Agent! till all shall be free,
O'er every nation and every sea.[23]

Standing in this tradition, the Revolt represents the continuity of God's purpose, speaking truth to power and the public role of Christian Religion. Otherwise put, grounding the Sam Sharpe Revolt in the Prophetic Tradition is not to spiritualize the event but to demonstrate that the same God who is revealed in the Prophetic Tradition is the same God who acted and was revealed in the Sam Sharpe Revolt in demanding liberation, justice and equality for the oppressed.[24]

As a theological act grounded in the Prophetic Tradition, the Sam Sharpe Revolt can be interpreted as a continuity of the purpose of God in history with particular significance for the liberation of the oppressed. Given that the social context of the prophets differed from that of Sam Sharpe's, there is continuity in terms of the experience of oppression and struggle for liberation. This continuity is a common thread that connects and intersects with the era of prophets to indicate that the Revolt was not merely socio-political but an essential expression or manifestation of God's will in history. As such, it is intended that this theological interpretation of the Sam Sharpe Revolt engenders the conviction and understanding that God's work which is revealed in the Prophetic Tradition will be acknowledged as a continuity of God's work in history.

Also, this perspective seeks to demonstrate that the Revolt affirms God's will for the liberation of all and makes a difference in society as it expresses the conviction that the same God who was revealed in the Prophetic Tradition is the same God who is active and present in the world today. In fact, it could be argued that the Sam Sharpe Revolt testifies to God's continued revelation in history.

Closely related to this purpose and the involvement of God in human affairs is the uncompromising and non-negotiable commitment of speaking truth to power as the Prophetic Tradition demonstrates. Speaking truth to power refers to the irresistible call and compulsion to proclaim in words and works the will of God to those in positions of power and to speak out against injustices to transform society. For this reason, attention must be given to some of the works of the prophets. Consider the message of Ezekiel, for example, as he prophesied against the corrupt leaders of his time: 'The people of the land practice extortion and commit robbery; they oppress the poor and needy and mistreat foreigners denying them justice' (Ezek. 22:29). The prophets in their outrage against corruption, showed the ideal to which the society should aspire. Isaiah prophesied:

> *Wash your hands; make yourselves clean; remove evil from your doings, from before your eyes; cease to do evil, learn to do good; seek justice, liberate the oppressed, defend the orphans, plead for the widow* (Isaiah 1:16–17).

The belief that speaking truth to power is a prophetic task undergirded the Sam Sharpe Revolt. The Revolt as an example of the application of this belief to the socio-political reality can be interpreted as the truth of God operating in human society and in the life of the oppressed or more precisely, speaking truth to power. This understanding of the Revolt is an added voice to the debate on the theological meaning of the Revolt but theologians have not given much attention to it as noted in introduction of this book.

A possible reason for this scant attention to the theological interpretation of the Sam Sharpe Revolt is the underestimation of the enslaved as may be recalled from the discussion in chapter one. What may have been forgotten is that the enslaved were agents of change and of their own liberation as Richard Hart's excellent study on the role the enslaved played in ensuring their liberation[25] has shown. Gayraud Wilmore concurs with this claim. In his *Black Religion and Black Radicalism*, for example, Wilmore advances a very powerful argument that enslaved and oppressed Blacks have always been the agents and have taken the initiative for their own liberation. He rightly notes:

> *Blacks have used Christianity not so much as it was delivered to them by racist white churches, but as its truth was authenticated to them in the experience of suffering and struggle, to reinforce an enculturated religious orientation and to produce an indigenous faith that emphasized dignity, freedom and human welfare.*[26]

The Sam Sharpe Revolt represents this reality and demonstrates what Latin American Liberation Theology defines as 'The Power of the Poor in History.'[27] The significance of the power of the poor has implications beyond its immediate context as it demonstrated an essential dimension of the power of the truth of God which is the faith of the oppressed.

In this sense, this Revolt contradicted the notion that faith is personal and private and has no role or relevance in public life.[28] The song, 'The Right Hand of God' is a vivid and powerful example of the public role of faith as speaking truth to power.

> *The right hand of God is writing in our land,*
> *Writing with power and love,*
> *Our conflicts and our fears, our triumphs and our tears are recorded by the right hand of God...*
>
> *The right hand of God is planting in our land,*
> *Planting seeds of freedom, hope and love,*
> *In these Caribbean lands...*[29]

Interpreted within the framework of the Sam Sharpe Revolt, this song demonstrates that with a powerful hand God entered human history to liberate the enslaved who received their liberation as good news. Thus, grounded in the Prophetic Tradition, the Revolt signifies God's will of liberation for the enslaved then, now and in the future. This then leads to the third testimony of the Biblical Witness, the Gospel of Jesus Christ, the foundation of the theological meaning of the Sam Sharpe Revolt.

The Gospel of Jesus Christ

Liberation, as with the Exodus Story and the Prophetic Tradition, is the essence of the gospel of Jesus Christ. In this sense, the Sam Sharpe Revolt evokes for Black liberation struggle the memory of the Exodus Story, exercises the power of the Prophetic Tradition and attests to the truth of the gospel of Jesus Christ. This is the good news of God's redemptive and liberating purpose as manifested through the person and work of Jesus Christ without whom there is no gospel. According to theologian James Cone, 'He is the Revelation of, the special disclosure of God and man [*humanity*], revealing who God is what his [God's] purpose for *man [humanity]* is.'[30] Cone's emphasis on the inseparability between Jesus and the gospel is also addressed in Dwight Hopkins' creative work, *Down, Up, and Over: Slave Religion and Black Theology.* His basic definition of the meaning of Jesus concisely captures this relationship:

> *Jesus is the Emmanuel – the decisive revelation of God with us. This revelation of the sacred with us occurs not in an abstract ethereal spirituality. In fact, Jesus' spirit appears with us in the macro, micro, linguistic, and racial cultural formations among the black poor and working people, and through them, the global poor.*[31]

The memory of the Exodus Story and the power of the Prophetic Tradition played a central role in shaping the identity and defining the mission of Jesus. For example, the account of the liberation of the youngster from an 'unclean spirit' identified as 'Legion' recalled the story of Pharaoh's defeat at the Red Sea (Exod. 14:1–31). Mark writes: 'And the unclean spirit…numbering about two thousand… rushed down to the steep bank into the sea and were drowned in the sea' (Mark 5:13). This account suggests that just as God entered into solidarity with the oppressed to ensure their liberation, so Jesus, epitomized this act of liberation through his person and ministry. And, this is the news of God's liberation of the enslaved, poor, oppressed and marginalized. As Luke reports:

> *The Spirit of the Lord is upon me because he has anointed me to preach the gospel to the poor. He has sent me to proclaim*

> *release to the captives and recovery of sight to the blind, to set at liberty those who are oppressed, to proclaim the acceptable year of the year (Luke 4:18–19).*

Clearly, in this inaugural sermon, Jesus stood within the Prophetic Tradition as he announced the dawn of God's Kingdom, established its time-frame, offered a model of life for humanity and revealed God's intent for the oppressed. This is a proclamation that encompasses the whole of life. He preached good news to the poor. These are those who lost the will, the desire and the strength to live due to social and spiritual powers of oppression. The proclamation of liberty suggests liberation from all that oppresses, which encompasses all aspects of life. Freedom for the captives connotes God setting free the poor and oppressed from all manner of imprisonment and hindrances in the pursuit of liberation.[32] More specifically, Jesus preached liberation, healed the sick, empowered the powerless and sided with the excluded, the marginalized and dehumanized. According to James Cone:

> *In Christ, God enters human affairs and takes side with the oppressed. Their suffering becomes his; their despair, divine despair. Through Christ the poor man [**person**] is offered freedom now to rebel against that which makes him other than human.*[33]

This remark is an example of the meaning of the gospel which the oppressed as in the case of the Sam Sharpe Revolt believed and accepted. They believed that God gave them the power to fight evil and to respond to this purpose of God by living in light of the freedom God offers and the kingdom Jesus inaugurated.

This remark is to affirm the view that Jesus embodied the gospel through his life and ministry. The works he performed were all about liberating people from oppression as he confronted the socio-political establishment of his time. It is in this sense that the enslaved identified with Jesus and the Sam Sharpe Revolt is considered to be grounded in the Gospel of Jesus Christ.

In their attempt to seek liberation, the oppressed also pledged their loyalty to Jesus as their only master. According to theologian Dwight Hopkins:

> *...Jesus, the Spirit of total liberation with us, offers one of the most freeing fruits of all: an emancipated status in this world where no other person, place, thing, or situation has absolute supremacy over those suffering. This beneficial effect liberates... the least and those at the bottom of the society to seek allegiance, not to earthly principalities and powers, but to the one with them along their journey to full humanity.*[34]

In particular, the Sam Sharpe Revolt is an example of the oppressed subverting the social order and carrying out what their acceptance of the gospel and allegiance to Jesus meant and empowered them to do, as was discussed in chapter three. Dwight Hopkins grasps this claim in his writing about the meaning of Jesus the Liberator of the enslaved. He states:

> *One cannot serve both the master that is the hegemony and influence of evil and the realm and righteousness of the master offering freedom to be free. Because the one master's (that is, Jesus') will emboldens the oppressed to seek their own pathway toward liberation and the practice of freedom, service to Jesus the one master with them implies the subservience of the poor to their own goal of liberation.*[35]

Premising the Sam Sharpe Revolt on the gospel of Jesus Christ requires that we ask what it means to confess faith in Jesus Christ in a particular historical context with its numerous and diverse issues. The meaning that emerges inspires a passionate engagement in the struggle and process of liberation that led the enslaved to reject unjust social structures and affirm the totality of God's redemptive and liberating purpose. An indication of the importance of the gospel to the Sam Sharpe Revolt and the extent to which the Revolt was rooted in the gospel is detected in the claim of James Cone concerning the meaning of Jesus Christ. Cone unapologetically writes:

> *...Jesus is the man for others, who views his existence as inexplicable apart from others. The others, of course, refers to all men* **[persons]**, *especially the oppressed, the unwanted of society, the 'sinners.' He is God himself coming into the very depths of human existence for the sole purpose of striking*

off chains of slavery, thereby freeing man ***[humanity]*** *from ungodly principalities and powers that hinder his relationship with God.*[36]

The Sam Sharpe Revolt is a radical strike at the heart of this unjust corrupt system of principalities and powers. It is radical in the sense that it confronted the root cause of the oppression of slavery which dehumanized, denied and prevented the enslaved from becoming what they ought to become. Thus, grounding the Revolt in the gospel of Jesus Christ demonstrates that it was God's act of judgment against the wicked and unjust system of slavery and oppression similar to the account of the liberation of the oppressed and the defeat of Pharaoh as recorded in the biblical story of the Exodus. In this account, it was God questioning, exposing and working to dismantle and to terminate the system of injustice and to liberate the oppressed. Essentially, the Sam Sharpe Revolt is an example of the response of the enslaved and oppressed when they heard the gospel. Fred Kennedy in his literary portrayal of the life of Sam Sharpe depicted the attitude of the enslaved towards the message of their liberation from slavery in the following manner:

We were becoming anxious to obtain freedom. Since the massas were not giving us what we wanted, we started going to church in even larger numbers to hear if the parson would give us the freedom message of Massa Christ.[37]

If the gospel is, indeed, liberation, then the Sam Sharpe Revolt gives voice to the voiceless and power to the powerless as the gospel becomes for them the power of God for salvation (Rom. 1:16). Along with the Exodus Story and the Prophetic Tradition, grounding the Sam Sharpe Revolt in the gospel of Jesus Christ, makes it a powerful tool and force for social transformation. The Jamaican Reggae Artiste, Bob Marley, in his pertinent awareness and prophetic vision, depicts this reality in the words of the song 'Small Axe.'

Why boasteth thyself, O, evil man
Playing smart and not being clever
I say you're working iniquity to achieve vanity
But the goodness of Jah Jah endureth forever

These are the words of my master
Keeping on telling me
No weak heart shall prosper
Whosever diggeth a pit, shall fall in it
And whosever diggeth a pit, bury in it
If you are a big tree, we are a small axe
Ready to cut you down.[38]

This song represents a revolution in the understanding of the oppressed. It is a revolution in faith and theology of the nature of the power of faith working in the oppressed. When the oppressed ground their faith in the Biblical Witness, there is no telling what they can do. What this suggests is that the God of the Biblical Witnesses is the same God at work in the world today.

Conclusion

This chapter attributes the liberation of the oppressed to themselves. It was an act of self-determination, refusal to continue living in oppression rooted in the Divine purpose of liberation attested to by the Biblical Witnesses. The discussion therefore raises questions about expecting or waiting for some kind of external messiahs to come and liberate the oppressed. Instead, we find affirmation of the power of the oppressed in Bob Marley's popular and influential song, 'Redemption Song.'

Emancipate yourselves from mental slavery,
None but ourselves can free our minds.
Have no fear for atomic energy,
'Cause none of them can stop the time.
How long shall they kill our prophets,
While we stand aside and look?
Some say it's just a part of it.
We've got to fulfill the book.[39]

The above stanza of this song speaks of oppressed as the ones who have the responsibility to liberate themselves. While the affirmation reiterates the power of the oppressed, the notion could obscure the source of power. Indeed, the oppressed have power but it is a gift from God through faith in Jesus Christ as indicated in the Biblical Witnesses.

What is distinctive about this power is not only the fact that it liberates but that it renews, restores and reconciles. In continuing the discussion, we examine next, the product of this power in history.

Notes

1. Henry Bleby, *Death Struggles of Slavery, 2nd ed.*, (London, 1868), 111.
2. Richard Hart, *Slaves Who Abolished Slavery: Blacks in Rebellion* (Kingston: University of the West Indies Press, 1985), 336.
3. Philip Sherlock & Hazel Bennett, *The Story of the Jamaican People* (Kingston: Ian Randle Publishers, 1998), 229–30.
4. John Howard Hinton, *Memoir of William Knibb, Missionary in Jamaica (1849)* (London: Houston and Stoneman, 1847).
5. Fitzer William Burchell, *Memoir of Thomas Burchell*, (London: Benjamin L. Green, 1849).
6. C. S. Reid, *Samuel Sharpe: From Slavery to National Hero* (Kingston: Bustamante Institute for Public and International Affairs, 1988), 4.
7. I am aware of the argument concerning the historicity of the Exodus Story. My usage of this account is as a paradigm in rejecting, resisting and revolting against oppression. Thus, the purpose or function of the Exodus Story is as a liberative tool which addresses oppressive hegemonic powers.
8. Noel Leo Erskine, *Decolonizing Theology: A Caribbean Perspective* (New York: Orbis Books, 1981), 77–81.
9. James Cone, *God of the Oppressed* (New York: Seabury Press, 1975), 63.
10. Cone, (1975), 62.
11. Allen D. Callahan, *The Talking Book: African American and the Bible* (New Haven: Yale University Press, 2006), 130. Although Callahan argues that there are similarities and differences between the experiences of enslaved Hebrew people and Blacks, referring to African Americans, their exodus is yet to come. I wonder if this is the case only for African Americans. Maybe, since the study, as the title of his book states, is about African Americans and the Bible and not the Black Diaspora.
12. Robert Beckford, *Dread and Pentecostal: A Political Theology for the Black Church in Britain* (London: Society for the Promoting Christian Knowledge, 2000), 98.
13. Miroslav Volf, *Exclusion & Embrace: A Theological Exploration of Identity, Otherness and Reconciliation* (Nashville: Abingdon Press, 1996), 9–31.
14. Noel Leo Erskine, *Black Theology and Pedagogy* (New York: Palgrave Macmillan, 2008), 121–34.

15. Laurie M. Cassidy and Alex Mikulich, eds., *Interpreting Whiteness: Catholic Theologians Break the Silence* (New York: Orbis Books, 2007).
16. Barbara Hilkert Andolsen, 'Social Justice, The Common Good and New Signs of Racism,' in *Interpreting White Privilege,* ed. Laurie M. Cassidy and Alex Mikulich (New York: Orbis Books, 2007), 58.
17. Ibid.
18. Erskine, *(208)*, 131.
19. Randall Bailey, 'The Biblical Basis for a Political Theology of Liberation,' in *Blow the Trumpet in Zion: Global Vision and Action for the* 21st *-Century Black Church*, ed. Iva E. Carruthers, Fredrick D. Haynes III and Jeremiah A. Wright, Jr. (Minneapolis: Fortress Press, 2005), 91–96.
20. James Cone, *Martin, Malcolm & America* (New York: Orbis Books, 1981).
21. Jim Wallis, *God's Politics: Why the Right Gets It Wrong and the Left Does not Get It* (New York: HarperCollins Publishers, 2005).
22. Walter Brueggemann, *The Prophetic Imagination* (Philadelphia: Fortress Press, 1978), 1–78; See also his, *Testimony to the Otherwise: The Witness of Elijah and Elisha* (Missouri: Chalice Press, 2001); *Hopeful Imagination: Prophetic Voices* (Philadelphia: Fortress Press, 1986). For an illuminating and refreshing study on Prophetic Tradition, see Obery M. Hendricks, Jr., *The Politics of Jesus: Rediscovering the True Revolutionary Nature of Jesus Teachings and How They Have Been Corrupted* (New York: Doubleday, 2006). Although not from the perspective of liberation theology, for an excellent study of the message of the prophets, see Gerhard von Rad, *The Message of the Prophets* (New York: Harper & Row, 1967).
23. Cited in Cawley St Clair Bolt, *Some Missing Understanding of Negro Characteristic in Jamaica, 1834–1870 with Particular Reference to Selected Baptist Missions.* (Ph. D. Thesis, Oxford Centre For Christian Missions, University of Wales, 2006), 119.
24. Desmond Tutu, *God Has A Dream: A Vision of Hope for Our Time* (New York: Doubleday, 2004).
25. Richard Hart, *Slaves Who Abolished Slavery: Blacks in Rebellion* (Kingston: University of the West Indies Press, 2002).
26. Gayraud Wilmore, *Black Religion and Black Radicalism: An Interpretation of the Religious History of Afro-American people* (New York: Orbis Books, 1983), 4.
27. For an in depth study on this subject, consult Gustavo Gutierrez, *The Power of the Poor in History* (New York: Orbis Book, 1983).
28. For an exemplary study on the role of faith as public witness, see Neville Callam, *Voicing Concerns: The Social Witness of the Jamaica Council of Churches* (Kingston: Pelican Publishers, 2004). See also, Anthony G.

Reddie, *Working Against the Grain: Re-imaging Black Theology in the 21st Century* (London: Equinox Publishing Ltd., 2009); Dwight Hopkins, ed., *Black Faith and Public Talk Critical Essays on James H. Cone's Black Theology & Black Power* (New York: Orbis Books, 1999).

29. Patrick Prescod, 'The Right Hand of God,' *Lift Every* Voice *and Sing II: An African American Hymnal* (New York: The Church Pension Fund, 1993), 61.
30. Cone, *Black Theology and Black Power* (New York: Harper & Row, 1969), 34.
31. Dwight N. Hopkins, *Down, Up, and Over: Slave Religion and Black Theology* (Minneapolis: Fortress Press, 2000), 193–94.
32. Hopkins, *Down, Up, and Over: Slave Religion and Black Theology,* 194–96.
33. Cone, (1969), 36.
34. Hopkins, 223.
35. Hopkins, 223–24.
36. Cone, (1969), 35.
37. Fred W. Kennedy, *Daddy Sharpe: A Narrative of the Life and Adventures of Samuel Sharpe, A West Indian Slave Written by Himself, 1832* (Kingston: Ian Randle Publishers, 2008), 213.
38. Robert N. Marley, *Small Axe.* Bob Marley and the Wailers, Prod. Direct Source Special Production Inc.
39. Robert N. Marley, *'Redemption Song,'* Bob Marley and the Wailers, Prod. Islands Record Inc., 1980.

7 - All O' We A One:
The Ties that Bind

INTRODUCTION

The factors that connect the Black Diaspora, the separated and scattered people of African ancestry throughout the world, but particularly those in the Caribbean, United Kingdom and the United States of America, are difficult to determine. Is it ancestry, ethnicity, history, culture, social conditions or faith that most adequately determines this link?

Taking into account that all of these factors have played a central role in connecting the Black Diaspora, the view is advanced that the faith in Jesus Christ as symbolized by the Sam Sharpe Revolt can function as a paradigm for connecting the Black Atlantic Diasporan people. Moreover, faith is not only a tool for enabling a deeper understanding of the theological dimensions of this relationship, but it is also an essential factor in the struggle for liberation and the quest for freedom.

As indicated above, the term Black Diaspora refers to the people of African heritage who have been shaped by slavery, colonialism and imperialism. Kortright Davis observes that the lives of these people are a story of:

> *The totality of the cultural traditions, organizations, institutions, and systems of oppressed people in their struggle for meaning, dignity, and a better life.* **[This experience is the persistent endeavour]** *of Caribbean, African American and* **[Black British]** *people to transform the meaning of slavery and oppression, poverty and dependence, failure and weakness, into powerful signs of promise, achievement, fulfilment, and historical emancipation.*[1]

Used in this sense, the term Black is not used in juxtaposition to White or Euro-American. Rather it identifies a particular people whose humanity is always in question and who have been dehumanized, alienated and separated from each other due to the slave trade and migration. Despite this experience, they have been a symbol of hope and have been able to bequeath to future generations a passion and respect for human life. Davis says it well:

> *Black denotes that dynamic spirituality of a particular type of people who have had the distinction of being the only ones in history whose claim to being human have been systematically called into question, in Europe, the Americas, the Caribbean and Southern Africa. It signifies the vitality of a people who have had to subsist culturally at the underground level but who passed on from generation to generation a quality of spirit that loved human life and dignity in the face of threatened extinction and overwhelming distinction. It is the sign of a people with a relentless trust in the future, in spite of the fact that they have been alienated from their ancestors, their inheritance, their land, their power.*[2]

Here, Davis has shown what Black people have become despite their experiences. But given the reality that slavery has broken the bond of kinship and separated us from each other, the common experiences of oppression and struggle for liberation from all forms of oppression in the context of a globalized world, then an effort to connect this disconnected people is warranted. To this effect, if liberation theologians, as indicated in chapter four are serious about the realization of God's purpose for the fullness of life for all persons and to provide an authentic response to the challenges of the disconnection among the Black Diaspora, then a discussion on the relationship of this Diaspora is long overdue.

Initiating this discussion, the issue is probed in order to identify some factors that can connect the Black Diaspora. Faith in Jesus Christ as expressed by the Sam Sharpe Revolt is employed as the interpretive framework for this relationship. Sharpe is important to this discussion in terms of his heritage as a person of African descent, a person who accepted and embodied the Christian faith and the theological and social implications of the Revolt he led against slavery. In interpreting this relationship, three dominant factors are identified, which derived from faith also connect the Black Diaspora in historical relations – a theological 'culturality' and a common quest for liberation and freedom. In each case, focus is placed on the theological dimension. There is a historical, theological and existential connection of the Black Diaspora.

Historical Relationship

A historical relationship based on kinship[3] and a covenant of faith connects the Black Diaspora. In the Black theological tradition, this relationship began with the establishment of the Black Church Tradition in the Caribbean by the African Americans, with George Liele in Jamaica, Frank Spence and Prince Williams in the Bahamas and William Hamilton in Trinidad and Tobago.[4]

Noel Erskine, in his seminal text on Caribbean theology, *Decolonizing Theology: A Caribbean Perspective,* advances this view based on the person and work of the African American preacher and pastor, George Liele. Liele was among the more than 5,000 people who migrated with their enslavers from the United States of America in 1883 to Jamaica in protest against the new form of government in the United States of America.[5] By the time of his arrival in Jamaica, he obtained his freedom from slavery but chose to maintain his relationship with his so-called owner, Henry Sharpe.[6] This slave owner permitted him to preach and conduct church services on the plantations. As Erskine confirms:

> *Once in Jamaica, Liele began to preach to black people there. This first black man to preach to black people in Jamaica took as the text for his first sermon Romans 10:1: 'Brethren, my heart's desire and prayer for Israel is that they might be saved. Liele compared the plight of black Jamaica to that of the children of Israel in Egypt.'*[7]

Liele's remark reveals that it was a fellow Black person, one of their own who brought the Christian message to the Black community to the Caribbean.[8] Since Christianity was brought to this community of people through this agency, it negates the notion that Christianity is the religion of Euro-American people. Proponents of this view fail to understand that Christianity originated in Africa and not in Europe or America.[9] Africans have played a crucial role in the development of Christianity.[10] For example, some of the decisive issues of Christianity including the doctrines of the Incarnation and the Trinity were determined by Africans such as by Athanasius of Alexandria[11] and St Augustine of Hippo,[12] respectively. Also, Africa played a pivotal role in expansion of the Christian Faith. David T. Shannon and Gayraud S.

Wilmore affirm this assertion in their, *Black Witness to the Apostolic Faith*. After defining the process of transmitting the faith from one generation to the next, these theologians made the claim more explicit:

> *We recognize, therefore, the apostolicity of what we received from our slave ancestors who, though they were 'unlearned and ignorant' men and women, reinterpreted the distorted Christianity they received from slave masters and passed down to succeeding generations of Black believers the story of Jesus who was 'the strong Deliverer,'...and the help of the poor and needy in this lan'...*[13]

In light of this understanding, the idea of kinship plays a central role as a means of connecting the Black Diaspora. The importance of kinship with all of its complexity is deployed here to demonstrate certain misconceptions of the relationship among the Black Diaspora. The intent is to offer an alternative perspective of kinship by grounding this relationship in faith.

The other factor of the historical relationship among the Black Diaspora is a covenantal commitment. Liele adopted and implemented a practice of church membership and social relationship based on the terms of a church covenant he adopted from the Euro-American church tradition which will be discussed later in this chapter. Covenant should be understood as the acceptance and commitment to live by a common set of beliefs and values delineated in a written religious document. In his work of organizing churches, Liele used this document as a tool for forging relationships within the Black community and also between the Black community and the Euro-American political and religious establishments. The following articles of the covenant express this intent:

> *We permit not slaves to join the church without first having a few lines from their owners of their good behaviour* (1 Peter 2:13–16).
>
> *If a slave or a servant misbehaves to their owners, they are to be dealt with according to the word of God* (1 Tim. 1:6; Eph. 6:5; 1 Peter 2:18–21; Titus 2:9–11).
>
> *We hold to all other Commandments, Articles, Covenants, and*

> *Ordinances, recorded in the Holy Scriptures, as are set forth by our Lord and Master, Jesus Christ, and his Apostles, which are not written in this Covenant, and to live to them as nigh as we possible can, agreeable to the word of God* (John 15:7–14).[14]

The contents of this covenant expressed the theological, moral and social functions of the church in the society. It could be argued that ethical concerns about relationship have a place in Black theological discourse and that it occupies a central dimension of what it means to be in relationship. On one hand, the implications of this practice signal how the covenant functioned as core values, statement of beliefs or confession of faith joined the people in a relationship.[15] On the other hand it raises the question that the covenant served to reinforce the institution of slavery rather than to transform the society from such wrong and evil.

With these unanswered questions, nevertheless, the origin of this form of covenantal relationship among the Black Diaspora is a matter of concern. Noel Erskine argues that the practice of establishing this kind of covenantal relationship in question originated in the United States.[16] Clement Gayle differs from Erskine's view arguing that this practice originated in Europe through the Free Church Tradition.[17] The issue, however, is not the place of origin of the covenant but the fact that it was grounded in the Euro-American church tradition. But then, it was through the covenant in terms of its mutual agreement among the African people and not the person George Liele who formed the bond or is the cord that binds diasporan Black people together.

The attraction of Black people to Christianity is another issue of concern. One wonders if the attraction of Blacks to this European version of Christianity could be due to its moral and ethical teachings as delineated in Liele's church covenant. However, a problem emerges when we postulate that European-derived ethics is the reason for Blacks to embrace their version of Christianity. It is general knowledge that Black people have their own ethical system.[18] Ethics in this instance involves commitment to the struggle of liberation and consequently departs from that of Euro-Americans as discussed in chapter four.

Notwithstanding this observation, this form of covenant-making can become problematic for the nature of theology being advocated.

Why did Liele and his colleagues establish relationships with a Euro-American tradition of the Christian faith? Was it because of loyalty to their British enslavers? Was this affinity to their enslavers a reflection of their religious sentiments and theological belief? How could they embrace a religious tradition that justified their oppression?

The oppressive character of the Euro-American religious tradition in question is not the Christianity of Jesus Christ.[19] Kelly Brown Douglas in her very helpful book, *What's Faith Got to Do with It?: Black Bodies and Christian Souls*, offers an illuminating account of the relationship between the Black experience and Christianity. She argues that the partnership between Christianity and Platonism created a tradition of oppression in Christian history and theology.[20] Tracing the development of the oppressive practices of Christianity, Douglas locates its origin in Greek philosophy which denigrated and demonized materiality which she calls a Platonized view of life. In Douglas's view, this understanding of life is defined by a dualistic cosmology which is an antithesis to Black Religion.[21]

As Douglas sets out to articulate some possible reasons Blacks became Christians, the question she seeks to answer has always been asked; why and how can Black people be Christians given Christianity's tradition of oppression of Blacks? After establishing the theological foundation for understanding the relationship between Christianity and Black people, Douglas proceeds to provide an alternative to the dominant Euro-American interpretation of Christianity. She is careful to point out that Euro-American Christianity became allied with Greek philosophy and political power to create a false religion which she defines as 'Platonized Christian tradition.'[22] This Euro-American version of Christianity advances a dichotomized worldview and justifies the dehumanization of Blackness.[23]

The commonalities between Christianity and Greek philosophy led to this dualistic version of religion. What are these commonalities? In the case of Christianity, the dualism is 'closed monotheism' and a 'Christological paradox' of the two natures of Jesus Christ.[24] Regarding Platonized Christianity, it makes a distinction between the soul and the body. According to Douglas, Platonized Christianity glorifies the concept of soul and denigrates the human body. Recognizing this distinction and proposing an alternative and by implication, a correct interpretation of Christianity, Douglas calls attention to one of the contributing factors in the de-humanization of the Black person.[25]

What Black people accept and believe is the notion of Jesus as the revelation of God in history, who is in solidarity with them.[26] Faith in this Jesus, Kelly Brown Douglas declares,

> *empowered and sustained black bodies under antagonistic social-historical conditions; it resonated with black people's deepest aspirations for life and dignity; and it reflected the continued presence of God in black people's life as informed by the biblical witness to God and their African theological heritage.*[27]

Douglas's argument indicates that faith in Jesus Christ is the central factor that attracts Black people to Christianity and explains why Black people are Christians. In the case of George Liele, Blacks allied themselves with the Euro-American version of Christianity for political reasons. As was discussed in chapter three, it was illegal for the Black community to practise their Christian faith and Liele was jailed for preaching.[28] In order for him to be able to carry out his ministry and establish Christianity among them, he took steps to forge a relationship with the political and religious authorities in two ways. In the first step, Liele sided with the plantocracy by teaching a religion that justified the status-quo which means he advanced a slaveholding Christianity. Second, he drafted and adopted a church covenant based on his compromised position which he presented to the government for certification[29] as indicated in the following statement of his church covenant: 'We bind ourselves, under an affirmation, to do duty to our king, country, and laws, to see that the affixed are duly observed.'[30]

Here, contrary to Douglas's argument why Blacks became Christians, this act of Liele underscores the claim that when Blacks allied themselves with the Euro-American version of Christianity, it was not necessarily because they wanted to become Christians but rather it should be viewed as a political act. Without this kind of alliance, it would not only be difficult but more dangerous for Black preachers of the time to preach and practise their Christian faith since it was illegal for them to do so.[31] The fact that Liele remained faithful in fulfilling his Christian vocation, demonstrates his political astuteness and theological acumen.

Liele's act further suggests that it is not on the basis of racial identity but in the crucible of oppression through the framework of historical consciousness that the relationship among the Black Diaspora has been forged.

What does this imply for Black religion? According to Erskine, it suggests that there are at least two possible paths to liberation within Black theological traditions[32] which is identified as the path of the God of the oppressor and the path leading to the God of the oppressed.[33]

Liele's relationship with the Euro-American Christian tradition on the one hand, represents the path of the God of the oppressor. This God justifies oppression and is for the rich and powerful. While this may suggest that Liele represents the God of the oppressor, which is debatable; it is more plausible to believe that he was pragmatic in his understanding of God as demonstrated in his alliance with the Euro-American ecclesiastical tradition.

The notion of God of the oppressed on the other hand, represents the path of Black religion, which the Native Baptists represent. They understand God to be on the side of the oppressed.[34] Although we have discussed in chapter three that the Native Baptists' religion departed from the tradition of Liele, it is worth mentioning that it is not clear if these two understandings of God co-existed in Liele's religious practice.

While Liele did not address the issue of slavery but preached an individualistic interpretation of the gospel of Christ, it is believed that the tradition of faith he established contributed to the Black liberation movement Sam Sharpe led. Clement Gayle conjectured that Liele's 'ministry served to raise the consciousness of those who were living under oppression and whose humanity was denied.' In Gayle's view, Liele's preaching of liberation from personal oppression was sure to create an awareness of physical oppression as the Sam Sharpe Revolt indicates.[35] For Gayle, Liele was not a Black liberation leader but he raised the consciousness of the need for liberation from oppression, established the relationship between the Jamaican Baptist and the British Baptist denominations which paved the way for the involvement of the latter in the country and exemplified a pattern of ministry that demonstrated the relationship between faith and education through the founding of schools.[36]

Theological Connection

Along with the kinship, theology also connects the Black Diaspora. On this basis, Kortright Davis's idea of intercultural theology as an expression of this connection is accepted. Davis defines this understanding of theology as,

> *the theological attempt to eliminate any need to rationalize any of our cultural biases, by striving relentlessly to reflect the sacramental dimension and universal character of the Christian faith while it is still conditioned by historical realities.*[37]

Davis is arguing that there is the need for a theology that takes into consideration the universal dimension of the Christian Faith and the social context that shapes it. Inter-cultural theology does not regard itself as absolute and is fully aware that it is socially and culturally conditioned.[38] As such, theologians attend to common themes in the Black experience as the constitutive elements of intercultural theology.[39]

Including the notion of the African Soul[40] and the experience of worship,[41] Davis argues that the telling of stories, exploring each other's history, celebrating common role models and participating in cultural practices are some of the themes of the Black Experience that bind the Black Diaspora. Defending this view, Davis writes: 'The Black Story is a continuing experience of Egypt – and the eternal religious truth is this: If you do not know your Egypt, you cannot know your Exodus.'[42] Thus, Davis's concept of Black theology includes the renewal of the common life, new expressions of liberation, advancement of the ecumenical purpose of the church, confronting the sin of racism, relating the Black experience to the biblical story, ensuring the continuity between theology and praxis, facilitating inter-religious dialogue and arguing that theology can provide the inspiration for solidarity.[43]

Adding to the cultural commonalities, Intercultural theology also consists of the common heritage, a common history of slavery and common experience of colonization, imperialism, migration and diasporan existence. Rex Nettleford, calls particular attention to this common heritage and experience:

> *This is severance from ancestral home whether it's from Africa, Europe, Lebanon, India, China, or the indigenous, Caribbean*

> *itself originally inhabited by Arawaks and Caribs. It constitutes suffering under enslavement, indentureship, and colonialism. It also constitutes* ***survival*** *and what exists beyond that survival...*[44]

Nettleford therefore, suggests that the common trauma of severance from ancestral heritage, the experience of suffering and acts of survival[45] of the Black Diaspora constitute the basis for establishing relationship among Black people. While these factors, however, may have defined the Black experience, without the element of faith in Jesus Christ, they are too tenuous and limited to form the basis for establishing relationship. This relationship would be based solely on negative experiences without attending to the positive aspects of the Black experience such as the practices, faith, justice, hope, inherent in their religion. At the same time, should the relationship be based solely on the positive as aspects of the Black experience, then, this would be romanticizing the Black experience.

Indeed, these two aspects, the positive and the negative, of Black life must be celebrated but not at the expense of each other. Both aspects of the experience are essential components of Black Diasporan life as expressed in the teachings of the Jamaican and international leader, Marcus Garvey.

A Garveyian vision of Black Diasporan relationship as another element of Intercultural theology. His insistence on Black unity and racial pride provided a path that could reconnect the relationship broken by slavery among Black people. Through the creation of the ideology of Black Nationalism, Garvey demonstrated his commitment to this view of relationship among the Black Diaspora. He indicated this in the following statements from the preamble of the constitution of the Universal Negro Improvement Association, the organization established 1 August 1914.

> *To establish a universal confraternity among the race [Black].*
>
> *To promote the spirit of race pride*
>
> *To reclaim the fallen race*
>
> *To establish universities, colleges and secondary schools for further education and culture of the boys and girls of the race.*[46]

The key to the above statement is the dynamic of Black unity. It also might bring to mind Garvey's extraordinary effort to promote Black Nationalism through his organization, various newspapers including *the Watchman* and the *Negro Word,* economic ventures such as The Black Star Liner and his eloquent discourses to inspire and connect the Black Diaspora. Garvey wrote:

> *But now we have reached the point where the entire race must get together... Whether we are light, yellow black or what not, there is but one thing for us to do, and that is to get together and build up a race. God made us in His image and he had some purpose when he thus created us.*[47]

Here much caution is required. This Garveyian assertion could potentially be accused of advancing the idea of Black cultural essentialism. This is the belief that certain characteristics such as ethnicity and nationality define Black people and if anyone does not belong to this heritage, they are considered different and excluded from the family of the Black Diaspora by their own people.[48] In this case, Intercultural theology could be regarded as hegemonic and exclusionary. Ironically, this is one of the challenges which Black theology faces or which it levels against others and seeks to intentionally avoid and dismantle. An underlying task of Intercultural theology is therefore to affirm the commonalities within the Black Diaspora but this is not the only approach to unite the Black Diaspora.

What is revealing about Intercultural theology is that it grounds relationship on the benefits that come from theology rather than on the theology itself. The goal of this theology is for solidarity and to demonstrate concrete expressions of freedom. The Caribbean intellectual tradition has long recognized the connectedness of the Black Diaspora through the common experience of heritage, slavery and the global system of capitalism. This view is represented in C.L.R. James's classic text, *The Black Jacobins*[49] and Eric Williams's classic work, *Capitalism and Slavery.*[50]

Regardless of how scholars interpret Williams's text, one might acknowledge his claim that slavery and the slave trade created the first global world, linking of the continents of Africa, Europe, North and South America.[51] In the case of James, he demonstrated that it was the enslaved who initiated, set in motion and dismantled this same system Euro-Americans created. Supporting this view, James advanced the idea that 'the Negro who came from Africa brought themselves[52] and he brought with him the contents of his mind, his memory. He thought in the logic and language of his people.'[53]

In view of such effort to provide a means for connecting a scattered people, Davis's proposal of an Intercultural theology is a creative resource. This effort is appreciated even though there is little agreement with the tools he uses to achieve the goal. Besides the urgent question whether cultural activities connect the Black Diaspora, the relationship is superficial without a theological meaning, interpreting the experience through faith in Jesus Christ. Also, with cultural activities, when used as theology, the goal is not an understanding of God who liberates and reconciles an oppressed, scattered and disconnected people. Rather, the goal is using culture as a source for constructing theology. Indeed, the issue in question is very complex. Recognizing this complexity, it is insisted that faith in Jesus Christ as Liberator is what gives this experience meaning and provides the source for connecting the Black Diaspora.

Interpreted from this perspective, the Black experience means that God in Jesus Christ is involved in the history and total experience of Black people as symbolized for example in the Sam Sharpe Revolt. This is to suggest that God is in solidarity with Black people and the liberating Jesus is to be found in the dislocation, fragmentation and disconnection of Black people. As such, if Intercultural theology is a means of connecting the Black Diaspora, it cannot ignore but rather, must address the realities of Black diasporan existence including the cause of migration, unjust immigration policies, underdevelopment of poorer countries, low wages, identity, fragmentation, alienation, separation, degradation, and the systemic structures that are designed by the 'powers that be' to inhibit the realization of human freedom. These realities are legitimately incorporated into the common quest for freedom which represents the final cord that connects the Black Diaspora.

Common Quest for Liberation and Freedom

The common quest for liberation and freedom is another dimension of faith which connects the Black Diaspora. This claim is predicated on liberation as the central theme of Black theology in the various contexts of the Black Diaspora, whether in the Unites States of America as African American theology and Womanist theology, in Great Britain as Black theology or in the Caribbean as Caribbean Liberation/Emancipatory theology. As essentially theologies of liberation, they are expressions of faith in the sense that Sam Sharpe applied his faith to the liberation struggle against slavery in the Revolt he led. Identifying, therefore, this expression of faith in the different context of Black theology is to demonstrate not only the interconnectedness of the Black Diaspora but the theological dimension of this relationship.

With the publication of James Cone's *For My People: Black Theology and the Black Church – Where Have We Been and Where are We Going,* we detect an initial acknowledgement that the Black Diaspora is connected through the common quest for freedom born out of the condition of oppression. He argues that liberation from oppression and the quest for freedom is the common struggle of oppressed peoples. Cone writes:

> *As white Americans, Europeans, South (**white**) Africans, and other oppressors band together in order to continue their rule over us, oppressed peoples throughout the world, across continents and nations, must band together for the liberation of all...It is a common struggle; there will be no freedom for any of us until all of us are set free.*[54]

Cone realizes that the oppressors are united in their programs to maintain and perpetrate oppression through futile ideologies and practices. Recognizing this unity, Cone emphasizes the need for doing theology from a global perspective of oppression. He proclaims: '…our mutual commitment to do theology in solidarity with the poor held us together.'[55] By this remark, Cone is correctly suggesting that rather than accepting the system of oppression and expecting the oppressor to terminate their evil practices and dismantle the inhumane system, the oppressed should unite in accepting their freedom in the struggle against oppression. This involves commitment, communication and cooperation. The purpose for this kind of Black unity is, as James Cone points out, 'to find ways to share our history and culture so that we can more effectively proclaim and practise together the liberating message of Jesus Christ.'[56]

The common quest for freedom transcends political ideology, religious beliefs and cultural differences. It is a theo-politico-ethical commitment to the poor. To this end, Cone writes:

> *We began to see the connection between the black ghettos in the United States and poverty in Asia, Africa, and Latin America; minorities in the USA and the exploitation of labor of Third World peoples; and between the racist practices of White churches of North America and Europe and the activities of their missionaries in the Third World.*[57]

The common quest for freedom takes into account the differences that exist among diasporan people. These differences are noted in the perspective from which Black theology is done. As Cone indicates:

> *Indeed they are First World enclaves in Third World countries in that they share the capitalistic values of white Americas and Europeans. The same is true among us in the USA who define freedom in terms of their equal share in the American capitalist pie with no thought whatsoever of changing the economic system so that the true cause of poverty could be eliminated not only in the USA but throughout the world. Therefore the chief characteristic that defined our concern was the commitment to do theology from the standpoint of our solidarity with the poor struggling for freedom.*[58]

This concern of Cone emerged from the particular context of the theologian and the people. It is questionable if African Americans are a people from a developing world. The uncritical acceptance of global capitalism and aspiration to conform to the status quo raise questions about the identity of Blacks in the United States and Britain. But then, the same question could be raised about those living in the developing world. They too have the same aspirations as their colleagues in these developed countries. In this regard, Cone correctly states: 'Third World [*Developing World*] referred to a condition of poverty and the struggle to overcome, and thus was not primarily or exclusively a geographical concept.'[59]

This common quest for liberation is also present in Black theology in Britain. Although not a study on the relationship among the Black Diasporan people, Anthony Reddie's, *Black Theology in Transatlantic Dialogue,* can be regarded as a voice for fostering this relationship. The study is an interpretive account of Black British theology in comparison with Black theology in the United States of America.[60] The significance of this work to the issue in question is Reddie's careful and insightful definition of the meaning of Black theology which he understands as interpreting the Christian faith through the lenses of the Black experience. He is unapologetic in his declaration:

> *When speaking of Black theology, I am referring to the specific self-named discipline of reinterpreting the Christian traditions and practices in light of liberationist themes and concepts, which arise out of the Black experiences.*[61]

In this view, Black theology is regarded as an intellectual discipline whose goal is the common quest for liberation and freedom. In this sense, liberation defines and interprets the Black experience. Black theology, then, presupposes commitment to liberation and transformation of society. Reddie makes this claim powerfully.

> *This approach is one that makes blackness and the black experience the initial point of departure (in partnership with Scripture, not Bible alone, as the sole authority) and uses these resources as the primarily hermeneutical lens by which the truth of God's liberating agency is discerned. In effect, blackness becomes the primary interpretive framework for reinterpreting and reimaging God and the Christian faith.*[62]

The reference to 'the Black experience' as the hermeneutical lens for interpreting the Christian faith is one of the major concerns of this chapter. For Reddie, Black theology in Britain takes seriously the theological meaning of the Black experience which serves as a tool for discovering God's liberating purpose. In this case, as with African American theology and Black theology in Britain, this quest for liberation is also the central theme in Caribbean liberation theology.

J. Emmette Weir's essay, 'Towards a Caribbean Liberation Theology' serves as an excellent example of this perspective of Caribbean theology. Weir expresses his view in the following remarks:

> *...there can be no doubt that a Caribbean Liberation Theology, like all other theological schools which is coming out of the Third World, should clearly be identified with the struggle of the poor and oppressed..., take most seriously its context..., begin with a careful analysis of its context...seek to be involved in the transformation of a society.*[63]

Burchell Taylor concurs with this view of Caribbean theology which he advances in his excellent article, 'The Theology of Liberation.' He writes:

> *The theology of liberation sees the search for understanding of what is taking place in historical context as part of getting to know and identifying with what God is doing in the outworking of his [God's] his liberative and redemptive purpose.*[64]

In the struggle for liberation and freedom, Taylor understands Caribbean Liberation Theology as a unifying factor within the Black Diaspora by identifying this quest as the act of God in history. This quest involves contextuality, practical, political and prophetic involvement, holistic orientation and a commitment to interpret the Christian faith including the Scripture in light of the existential realities.[65]

These claims are not to suggest that Black life is reduced, limited or held captive to struggles in life. Rather, it is to demonstrate that the relationship takes place in history or in a particular social context. Allan Kirton puts it succinctly; social context 'is the arena of God's activity and the theatre of human response.'[66] As such, the quest for liberation and freedom are existential realities serving Black people. Noel Erskine convincingly speaks to this idea in his *Decolonizing Theology.* He writes:

> *When one listens to the cry that resounds from the oppressed in Africa, the Caribbean, Latin America, Asia or North America, this longing for freedom is expressed as the central theme of their theologies.*[67]

In the context of the quest for freedom, these people encountered the liberating God who made it known that they were made for freedom[68] (Gal. 5:1). For Erskine then, the quest for freedom is the unifying principle among oppressed peoples which in this discussion refers to the Black Diaspora.

Womanist theology recognizes the common quest for freedom and proposes the path for forging such relationship. As a theology that advocates the survival and wholeness of the entire Black community,[69] it considers the Black community as a family. Writing in this regard, Kelly Brown Douglas grounds this notion of relationship on the doctrine of the Trinity. She recognizes the disagreements and problematic nature of this doctrine but nevertheless insists that 'it attests that the God of life and wholeness is internally and externally relational.'[70] Human beings made in the image of God reflect this character of God through relationships. Douglas writes clearly: 'Challenge by the faith of enslaved Africans, to be in the image of God is for us to be in relations of mutuality as we strive for life and wholeness.'[71]

While there is some agreement with Douglas's view on the importance of the relationship among Black people, it should also be considered what difference it would make if the relationship was not based on the problems in the Black community. Is it the crisis that determines the need for the relationship? Unless, she understands that human will, which rejects God's will of fullness of life for all persons, is behind this crisis. If this is not the case, then Womanist theology would be only responding to a crisis in the Black community. If crisis, therefore, is the reason for Womanist theology, then it would only be a reactive phenomenon and not a liberating intellectual discipline.

At the same time, the charge could be made that Womanist theology is the product of African American women which makes it insular and parochial. Its holistic character, however, transcends its context. In fact, its holistic nature is what makes it relevant and applicable to the Black Diaspora. Countering this charge is the holistic character of this theology. As Delores Williams points out:

> *Womanist theology is informed by at least four elements: (1) a multi-dialogical intent, (2) a liturgical intent, (3) a didactic, and (4) a commitment both to reason and to the validity of female imagery and metaphorical language in the construction of theological statements.*[72]

Additionally, the concept of family, as mentioned earlier in this discussion, transforms the idea of blood relations into a sense of peoplehood. Womanist theology embodied Black diasporan peoplehood through the vocation of caring for all and as agents of culture and working for the common good.[73] In this sense, Womanist theology incorporates not only the common quest for liberation and freedom but also Black theology throughout the Black Diaspora. Here, we are seeing evidence of the Black Diaspora taking responsibility for reordering God's world for the good of humanity.

Conclusion

The discussion so far has shown that there is no coherent, collective and systematic theological analysis of the relationship among the Black Diasporan. Rife with divisions and differences due, in many respects, but not limited to location, socialization and self-understanding, the time is not only ripe but it is the right thing to do. The effort is initiated at least to all for a discussion on this important issue. In this regard, the theological dimension of the relationship is explored by attending to the historical, theological and existential factors that connect the Black Diaspora.

Employing faith in Jesus Christ as the tool for probing the theological dimensions of this relationship identifies a resource for connecting a disconnected people. It further demonstrates that relationships are an essential dimension of freedom and justice. As the Sam Sharpe Revolt indicates, we recognize not only the unifying principle of faith but also when faith is applied to social reality, it dismantles any system of injustice and liberates the oppressed for freedom. What this implies about God, humanity and society or for Black theology is addressed in the next chapter.

Notes

1. Kortright Davis, *Emancipation Still Comin': Explorations in Caribbean Emancipatory Theology* (New York: Orbis Books, 1990), 118.
2. Ibid. Black identity is a problematic issue and has been sufficiently addressed by various scholars. Also, I have lent my voice to the discussion elsewhere. My intent in this discussion is not to solve nor complicate the problem. I am only calling attention to my usage of the

term. For further study on this issue, see Delroy A. Reid-Salmon, *Home Away from Home: The Caribbean Diasporan Church in the Black Atlantic Tradition* (London: Equinox Publishing Ltd., 2008) 29–75; Gwendolyn Midlo Hall, *Slavery and African Ethnicities in the Americas* (Kingston: Ian Randle Publishers, 2006) especially, 55–79; Michelle M. Wright, *Becoming Black: Creating Identity in the African Diaspora* (North Carolina: Duke University Press, 2004); Paul Gilroy, *Black Atlantic: Modernity and Double Consciousness* (Massachusetts: Harvard University Press, 1993); Darlene Clark Hine and Jacqueline McLeod, eds., *Crossing Boundaries: Comparative History of Black People in Diaspora* (Indianapolis: Indiana University Press, 1999), 3–175; Frantz Fanon, *Black Skin White Mask* (New York: Grove Press,1967).

3. Peter J. Paris, *The Spirituality of African People: The Search for Moral Ground* (Minneapolis: Fortress, 1995), 51–127. While Paris speaks of African peoples, the work addresses African Americans. However, I take the liberty to enlarge his audience to include the Black Diaspora.
4. Clement Gayle, *George Liele: Pioneer Missionary to Jamaica* (Kingston: Jamaica Baptist Union, 1982), 37–38.
5. Erskine, 41.
6. Gayle, 9.
7. Erskine, 42.
8. Gayle, 3; See also, E. A. Payne, 'Baptist Work in Jamaica before the Missionaries,' *The Baptist Quarterly* 7 (1934–35): 20–26; Shirley C. Gordon, *God Almighty Made Me Free: Christianity in Preemancipation Jamaica* (Bloomington & Indianapolis: Indiana University, 1996).
9. J. Deotis Roberts, *Africentric Christianity: A Theological Appraisal for Ministry* (Valley Forge: Judson Press, 2000).
10. Thomas C. Oden, *How African Shaped the Christian Mind: Rediscovering the African Seedbed of Western Christianity* (Illinois: IVP Books, 2008). This volume comes from a leading theologian who was schooled in the intellectual tradition that is predicated on the mistaken notion that Christianity is Western creation. This work is both an admission of centuries of error and an acknowledgement of what Western theological tradition denied. For further inquiry, see Mark Ellingston, *The Richness of St Augustine: His Contextual Pastoral Theology* (Kentucky: Westminster John Knox Press, 2005); Michael Joseph Brown, *The Lord's Prayer through North African Eyes: A Window into Early Christianity* (London: T&T Clark, 2004); A. Okechukwu Ogbonnaya, *On Communitarian Divinity: An African Interpretation of Trinity* (Minneapolis: Paragon House, 1998); Jeremiah Wright, *African Who Shaped our Faith* (Illinois:

Urban Ministries Inc., 1995).

11. Justo L. Gonzalez, *The Story of Christianity: The Early Church to the dawn of the Reformation* Vol.1 (Massachusetts; Prince Press, 1984), 173–88; For a study on the life of Athanasius, see Alvyn Petersen, *Athanasius* (Pennsylvania: Morehouse Publishing, 1995).
12. Gonzalez, 207–16; See also, Edmund Hill, translator, *Saint Augustine, The Trinity,* (New York: New City Press, 1991).
13. David T. Shannon and Gayraud S. Wilmore, *Black Witness to the Apostolic Faith* (Michigan: Eerdmans, 1985), 69.
14. 'The Covenant of the Anabaptist Church,' cited in *George Liele: Pioneer Missionary to Jamaica,* Clement Gayle (Kingston: Jamaica Baptist Union, 1982), 45.
15. Gayle, 33.
16. Erskine, 43.
17. Gayle, 33–35.
18. Cheryl Sanders, *Empowering Ethics for a Liberating People: A Path to African American Social Transformation* (Minneapolis: Fortress Press, 1995); Peter Paris, *The Spirituality of African Peoples: The Search for a Common Moral Discourse,* (Minneapolis: Fortress Press, 1995); Theodore Walker, *Empower The People: Social Ethics for the African-American Church* (New York: Orbis Books, 1991).
19. James Cone, *Black Theology & Black Power* (New York: Harper & Row Publishers, 1969), 62–115.
20. Kelly Brown Douglas, *What's Faith God to Do with It?: Black Bodies/ Christian Souls* (New York: Orbis Books, 2005), xiv.
21. Winston A. Lawson, *Religion and Race: African and European Roots in Conflict – A Jamaican Testament* (New York: Peter Lang Publishing, 1996), 4–56.
22. Douglas, 3–38.
23. Douglas, 3–106.
24. Douglas, 39–70.
25. Douglas, 150–98.
26. See James Cone, *God of the Oppressed* (New York: Seabury Press, Inc., 1975), 108–162; Dwight Hopkins, Down, *Up, and Over: Slave Religion and Black Theology* (Minneapolis: Fortress Press, 2000), 193–236.
27. Douglas, 201.
28. Erskine, 42.
29. Ibid.
30. Cited in Erskine, 42.
31. Ibid.

32. Erskine, 44.
33. James Cone, (1975), 128–46.
34. Erskine, 44.
35. Gayle, 39.
36. Gayle, 38–39.
37. Davis, 125. For a discussion on the theological perspective of culture, see Dwight Hopkins, *Being Human: Race, Culture, Religion* (Minneapolis: Fortress Press, 2005), 53–80.
38. See Lewin Williams, *Caribbean Theology* (New York: Peter Lang, 1994). For an explanation of this approach to doing theology, see Emmanuel Lartey, *In Living Colour: An Intercultural Approach to Pastoral Care and Counselling* (London: Jessica Kingsley, 2003).
39. Davis, 124. See also Emmanuel Lartey, *In Living Colour: An Intercultural Approach to Pastoral Care and Counseling* (London: Jessica Kingsley, 2003), 21–35.
40. Davis, 55–57.
41. Davis, 105–16.
42. Davis, 129.
43. Davis, 125–26.
44. Rex Nettleford, *Inward Stretch Outward Reach: A Voice from the Caribbean*, (London: Macmillan Press, 1993), 173.
45. Nettleford, 173–81.
46. Cited in Judith Stein, *The World of Marcus Garvey: Race and Class in Modern Society*, (Baton Rouge: Louisiana University Press, 1986), 30.
47. Marcus Garvey, *Philosophy & Opinion of Marcus Garvey, Vol. 11*, ed., Amy Jacques Garvey (New York: Antheneum, 1980), 60.
48. Victor Anderson, *Beyond Ontological Blackness: An Essay on African American Religious and Cultural Criticism* (New York: Continuum, 1995).
49. Eric Williams, *Capitalism and Slavery* (North Carolina: University of North Carolina Press, 1944), 30.
50. C.L.R. James, 'The Making of the Caribbean People,' in *Spheres of Existence* (London: Allison & Busby, 1980), 174.
51. James, 'The Atlantic Slave Trade,' in *The Future Present* (London: Allison & Busby, 1977), 243.
52. James Cone, *For My People: Black Theology and the Black Church – Where have We been and Where are We Going?* (New York: Orbis Books, 1984), 142.
53. Cone, (1984), 147.
54. Cone, (1984), 143–44.
55. Cone, (1984), 146.
56. Cone, (1984), 146–47.

57. Cone, (1984), 145.
58. Anthony G. Reddie, *Black Theology in Transatlantic Dialogue* (New York: Palgrave Macmillan, 2006), 2.
59. Reddie, 17. Reddie goes to great extent to define what he means by Black theology. In addition to Black theology, he identifies two different approaches (Colour Blind and Black Christian Religious Experience) of interpreting the Christian faith within the Black Christian tradition in Britain. For an exploration of this subject, see his *Working against the Grain: Re-Imaging Black Theology in the 21st Century* (London: Equinox Publishing Ltd., 2008), 1–29.
60. Ibid.
61. Emmette Weir, 'Towards a Caribbean Liberation Theology,' *Caribbean Journal of Religious Studies* 12, no. 1 (April, 1991): 45–46. Caribbean Liberation Theology is one model of Caribbean theology. For a representative a study on the different models of this theology, see Howard Gregory, ed. *Caribbean Theology: Preparing for the Challenges Ahead* (Kingston: Canoe Press, 1995); Lewin Williams, *Caribbean Theology* (New York: Peter Lang, 1994); Kortright Davis, *Emancipation still Comin': Explorations in Caribbean Emancipation Theology* (New York: Orbis Books, 1990); Noel L. Erskine, *Decolonizing Theology: A Caribbean Perspective* (New York: Orbis Book, 1981); Idris Hamid, *Out of the Depths* (San Fernando: St Andrew Theological College, 1977); For helpful discussion on the stages of development in Caribbean Theology, see Allan Kirton, 'Current Trends in Caribbean Theology and the Role of the Church,' *Caribbean Quarterly* 37, no. 1 (March 1991): 99–107.
62. Burchell Taylor, 'Theology of Liberation,' *Caribbean Quarterly* 37, no. 1 (March 1991): 25.
63. Taylor, 21–33.
64. Allan Kirton, 'Current Trends in Caribbean Theology and the Role of the Church,' *Caribbean Quarterly* 37, no. 1 (March 1991): 98–107.
65. Noel Leo Erskine, *Decolonizing Theology: A Caribbean Perspective* (New York: Orbis Books, 1981), 1.
66. Erskine, 1. See also, Phillip Potter and Barbel Wartenberg-Potter, *Freedom is for Freeing* (New York: United Methodist Church, 1990), 71–84.
67. Consult Delores S. Williams, *Sisters in the Wilderness: The Challenge of Womanist God-Talk* (New York: Orbis Books, 1994); Katie Geneva Canon, *Katie's Canon: Womanist and the Soul of the Black Community* (New York: Continuum, 1996).

68. Douglas, 77.
69. Ibid.
70. Delores Williams, 'Womanist Theology: Black Women's Voices,' in *Black Theology: A Documentary History, 1980–1992*, ed. James Cone and Gayraud Wilmore (New York: Orbis Books, 1993), 269.
71. Kelly Brown Douglas, 'To Reflect the Image of God' in *Living the Intersection: Womanism and* Afrocentrism *in Theology* (Minneapolis: Fortress Press, 1995), 67–77.
72. Delores Williams, 'Womanist Theology: Black Women's Voices,' in *Black Theology: A Documentary History Volume 2: 1980–92*, eds., James H. Cone & Gayraud S. Wilmore (New York: Orbis Books, 1993), 269.
73. Williams, 270.

8 - Fighting For Survival: Towards a Theology of the Black Atlantic Struggle for Liberation

INTRODUCTION

There are diverse understandings of the Sam Sharpe Revolt. As discussed in chapter two, some argue that it was a religious war. Others say it was a political event. There are still those who contend that it was an example of industrial action or social protest that resulted in a violent revolution.[1] With this depiction of the Sam Sharpe Revolt, we come to the heart of the discussion. What is the relevance and legacy of this act? What does theology in general and Black theology in particular have to say about this Revolt? What does this act mean for us today? In this regard, resides the reason to provide a theological meaning of this Revolt.

As an initial effort towards this endeavour and as well as an alternative to the previously discussed descriptive interpretations of the Sam Sharpe Revolt, I argue that this Revolt is a theological act signifying the revelation and involvement of God in history. This revelation takes the form of freedom, righteousness and hope.

Freedom

Theologically understood, the Sam Sharpe Revolt means freedom. Mention has already been made regarding the meaning of the term freedom in chapter four. In that discussion, freedom was considered as a constitutive element of the human being but will be alluded to in an attempt to define the theological meaning of the Sam Sharpe Revolt. What is intended in continuing the discussion is to express that while the term is understood as a core belief of the faith tradition of Sam Sharpe, it is also a revelation of persons becoming what God intended them to become. More precisely said, the Sam Sharpe Revolt is a visible manifestation, a tangible expression, a living embodiment and practical demonstration of God's will for the fullness of life for humanity that is demonstrated in the life and ministry of Jesus Christ.

Implicit in the notion of freedom is the revolutionary concept that human beings are made for freedom. As such, the Revolt is a rejection and renunciation of all forms of domination, degradation and dehumanization of people. Through this Revolt, the enslaved exercised the Divine right to be free and reclaimed control over their lives and destiny. The Revolt represented their collective will and defiant spirit. The Methodist missionary, Henry Bleby reported the following testimony of the enslaved as they prepared to do everything necessary to obtain freedom. 'We have worked enough already because the life we live is…the life of a dog. We won't be slaves no more, we won't lift hoe no more; we won't take flog no more. We free now; no more slaves again.'[2]

This human struggle is a response of the enslaved to God's will of freedom that is revealed in Jesus Christ. Jesus revealed God's will in history and points away from himself to the God whose nature is freedom and is the source of freedom. Writing about the theological meaning of this freedom, Kortright Davis expresses the belief that it is a gift from God.[3] He grounds his argument on the premise that God is sovereign, meaning a being who is the absolute and ultimate source of all authority and power and accountable to no other[4] but is in solidarity with the oppressed. Therefore, the notion of Divine sovereignty means that God is known in relation to persons but especially the most vulnerable, dehumanized, degraded exploited and downtrodden.

Indeed, the struggle for liberation is not God but is dependent on God. Davis, affirming this perspective, says it concisely: 'Divine sovereignty spells divine freedom.'[5] Theologians, therefore, must guard against making the error of equating God with liberation or practising an ideology of creating a God in our own image. Davis warns: 'At times in history of the West, the sovereign God has been made to look less than sovereign…In the final analysis, Christians either behave as if they believe that humanity is created in the image of God, or else they practice an ideology which affirms that God is merely an image of human creativity.'[6]

Noel Erskine, in his seminal text on Caribbean theology, *Decolonizing Theology: A Caribbean Perspective*, points out that there is a distinction between Divine and human freedom. He argues that human freedom is premised on Divine freedom to advance the notion that human freedom is both a response to, and a participation in Divine freedom.

Erskine puts this succinctly:

> *To respond to God's freedom is to recognize that historical freedom is a task which opens people up to divine freedom in which they encounter the transcendent in history. To participate in divine freedom is to offer to one the possibility to be free and to discover alternate ways to be human.*[7]

In this view, the oppressed take responsibility for their freedom and do whatever is necessary to ensure that freedom becomes a reality. At the same time, the oppressed believe that oppression is not only contradictory to God's will but also that if they do not fight against it they will never experience freedom.[8] Erskine explains:

> *When human freedom encounters divine freedom, the creation of a new humanity occurs. It is to become part of the realization that God's mission in the world is the creation of a new human. History then becomes the context in which this possibility of being human is realized.*[9]

Although freedom is made real in history, it is not dependent on human resolve and resources nor are human beings creating their own life and destiny. Injustices, certainly are manifestations of both the personal and collective will of human beings which resist, reject and rebel against God's will.[10] In response to Divine freedom, however, human beings may, as in the case of the Sam Sharpe Revolt, take responsibility for reordering society according to God's will. Undergirding this perspective is the conviction that freedom is a Divine right, thus it is right to fight for freedom. Failing to do so is to 'run the risk of forfeiting [our] ontological vocation to be free in history and [our place in the kingdom of freedom and humanity.'[11]

It is in this regard that the Sam Sharpe Revolt demonstrates that freedom is the goal and inspiration of liberation. The Revolt also shows that the destiny of the oppressed is not determined by the laws of the land but by God's will of liberation.

Righteousness

In addition to freedom, the Sam Sharpe Revolt can be theologically understood as an act of righteousness. The term righteousness is used not to describe the being of God but as the will of God to right the wrongs that human beings have done in the world. As theologian James Cones puts it: 'Righteousness is doing justice. He [*God*] is putting right what men [*human beings*] have made wrong.'[12] In Cone's view, God is acting in human history to effect the Divine purpose without regard to any form of opposition.[13] This view is consistent with the Biblical Witness as discussed in chapter five. This notion of righteousness as God's will of liberation for humanity but especially, the poor and the oppressed is undefeatable and indestructible. In the case of the enslaved, Divine righteousness is woven in the deep recesses of their beings and embedded in the fabric of their consciousness.

In this sense, Sharpe was convinced that leading the Revolt against the sin of slavery and oppression was an act of righteousness. He expressed this understanding of his action in the explanation he gave to the Methodist clergyman, Henry Bleby. When Bleby asked him about the reason for leading the Revolt, Sharpe replied by making it known that it was not an act of violence but an act of righteousness. According to Bleby, Sharpe expressed deep regret that such an extensive destruction of property and life had resulted from the Revolt but declared that this formed no part of his plan. He did not wish to destroy the estates, nor desire that any person should be injured; his only object was to obtain freedom.[14] This remark is compelling. Whereas it explains that Sharpe did not advocate violence, it expressed his deep belief in and his passionate intent to obtain freedom. He certainly was not presenting himself as a paragon of virtue but was compelled by his conscience, out of a sense of what was right, to act.

The Revolt also was a righteous act because the 'legitimate' means of administering justice, which in this case, the government of the country, was not doing what was right. For this reason, the Revolt was the best alternative available to the enslaved and oppressed to procure their freedom. Reflecting on Sharpe's Revolt as an act of righteousness, C.S. Reid argues that it was an act of conscience.[15] He defines the Revolt as 'The Relevance of Conscience' by calling attention to the appropriate alternative to take when the acceptable means fail to do what it was created to do. Reid explains that there is a tradition of Freedom Fighters that chose alternative means to obtain freedom when none exists.

Reid places Sharpe within this distinguished tradition. He concludes that the Revolt was in pursuit of freedom and these revolutionaries 'acted in the interests of high principles and humanity.'[16] According to Reid:

> *Sam Sharpe, the Baptist Deacon initiated a conspiracy to strike a blow at the monster of slavery. He paid with his life. But because we now recognize the true value of the freedom for which he died, we have given him our highest honor. The perspective of history has legitimized his conduct.*[17]

In spite of this high regard for Sharpe, however, we should not overlook or minimize the difficulty Sharpe may have experienced in determining the righteousness of his action. Reid nevertheless offers a brilliant insight into Sharpe's action when he describes the planning of the Revolt as an 'agonizing question of conscience.'[18]

Indeed, the demands of the Gospel as discussed in chapter five and the law of conscience as Reid now argues warrant action against injustice. Here Reid is very helpful. After he describes the historical context of the Sam Sharpe Revolt, he points out that teaching of the Christian Faith contracted and clashed with the values of the society. This contradiction of values was a moral issue. Here Reid addresses this moral dilemma by regarding Sharpe as symbol of the Christian Faith as well as a 'man [*person]* of conscience in an unjust society.'[19] Sharpe epitomizes this view when he said on the day of his execution that 'all I wished was to be free; all I wanted was to enjoy that liberty which I found in the Bible as the birthright of every man [human being].'[20]

Sharpe definitely was not a rebel in the sense of disregarding the law of the land but one who 'fought for his freedom.'[21] Indeed, Sharpe knew that his action was against the law of the land but he also knew and was thoroughly convinced that he did not violate God's law. The law of God for Sharpe was the law of Scripture. If, as Clarence Reid argues, Sharpe acted on the basis of his conscience, then the law of conscience (Rom. 2:15) is this same law of Scripture. Put otherwise, the law of Scripture is written on human conscience as indicated in Sharpe's words from the gallows, his cross; 'I have sinned against the laws of my country, and by those laws, I ought to die; But I cannot see that I sinned against my God.'[22]

This remark suggests that while Sharpe agreed that the Revolt violated human law, it does not mean that such law was just. One therefore could argue that his execution and the consequences he suffered for revolting against slavery were unjust. But such actions by the British government only go to confirm the Revolt as an act of righteousness. Moreover, it further indicates that the Revolt was based on God's law. This idea of righteousness resonates with the action of the first Apostles in their declaration to obey God's law which supersedes any law that contradicts it. The Apostles declared to the Roman government who offered them the option to refrain from preaching the gospel of Jesus Christ or be persecuted for doing so said: 'We must obey God rather than [*human beings*] man'(Acts 5:28–29; 4:18–21).

Certainly, for Sharpe, the Revolt was obedience to the law of God which transcended human law. It demonstrated loyalty to a higher law. His execution, therefore, was an expression of the unjust system and society. In explaining, for instance, the motive for igniting the fire to initiate the Revolt, the enslaved female servant who carried out such a bold act, is reported to have said: 'I know I will die for it but I did it so that my children will be free.'[23] By this statement, this female enslaved servant concurred with Sharpe that Revolt did not violate God's law and that she would pay the ultimate price for participating in it. She brought an added perspective to the theological understanding of the Sam Sharpe Revolt not only as an act of righteousness but as a prophetic and eschatological act by premising it on the implications for future generations. Otherwise put, it is reasonable to argue that with the intent to achieve freedom, this act of the enslaved woman who lit the fire, epitomized the Revolt in that it expresses God's will of freedom, righteousness and also hope, which will be discussed later in this chapter, for humanity.

The response of the enslaved to the missionaries' denial of the King of England granting them their freedom is another underscoring principle of Sam Sharpe and his fellow Freedom Fighters' commitment to the law of God. The enslaved were thoroughly convinced of the righteousness of the Revolt as indicated in their response to Knibb concerning the veracity of the news about their freedom.

At the dedicatory service of the Salter's Hill Church, in the parish of St James, Knibb called attention to the news that was circulating among the enslaved concerning their freedom. Knibb told them that it was not true that the King of Britain had granted them freedom so the news they heard was wrong.[24] After hearing such remark, the enslaved not only resented Knibb but they denounced him and all who opposed their freedom. The enslaved concluded that Knibb was insane to be telling them that they were not free.[25] Writing of this experience, the Presbyterian clergyman, Hope Waddell's description is insightful:

> *His assurances that no 'free law' had come, were discredited by the assembled thousands – his exhortations to be quiet and return to their estate duties enraged them. He never thought to see the people so furious; they accused their minister of deserting them; and the immediate destruction of all the properties in the surrounding districts was their fierce reply to his admonitions.*[26]

Expressing the same view as Knibb's to the members of his congregation, Waddell received from them a similar response. 'The people were not pleased with this address. Many looked downcast and disappointed; and they left the church, said one to another, minister give against we.'[27]

While the enslaved were disappointed with their pastors, Knibb and Waddell, who they felt betrayed them, they were not deterred from revolting. Instead, Knibb and Waddell's advice only confirmed the slaves' long held belief the British government granted freedom which the plantocracy refrained from implementing[28] and intensified their resolve to take their freedom, underscoring the rightness of their action. As Sharpe advised them; 'if the black men did not stand up for themselves, and take their freedom, the whites would put them in muzzles of their gun, and shoot them like pigeons.'[29]

The defence of the Revolt by the British missionaries as represented by William Knibb also attests to the theological understanding of the Sam Sharpe Revolt as an act of righteousness. Knibb exemplified this assertion in arguing that the reason for Sharpe's execution and the vicious and brutal persecution that resulted from the Revolt had nothing to do with the illegality of the Revolt, but had a lot to do with the colour of his skin. Knibb boldly declares:

> *...If Samuel Sharpe had been a Polish nobleman, and had taken the same measures to free the Poles from the grasp of*

the Russians as he took to free his countrymen from the unjust grasp of the slave owner, many in England would say, that, instead of being considered a rebel he deserved an imperishable monument.[30]

In this declaration, Knibb identified with Sharpe's action and at the same time, he affirmed the kinship of all persons. For Knibb, and correctly so, all persons are God's creation and on this basis, all human beings are related. As the Scripture declares; 'We are God's off-springs' (Acts 16:28). As to the theological interpretation of the Sam Sharpe Revolt as an act of righteousness, Knibb's understanding is quite straight forward. His belief in the parenthood of God and kinship of all persons is the primary reason he opposed slavery and defended the enslaved. He declares:

...here I will lift up my voice for injured Africa; and all I claim shall be that my African brother [and sister] may stand in the family of man [humanity]; my African sister may call her child her own; and that both may have free permission to bow their knees at the footstool of that God who has made of one blood all nations that stand on the face of the earth.[31]

Knibb, in interpreting slavery as a theological issue, further confirms the Sam Sharpe Revolt as an act of righteousness. The sin of slavery contradicts God's law of love and dehumanizes human beings which not only expresses injustice but also the rightness of that which opposes it as in the case of the Sam Sharpe Revolt. This sin took the form of beatings, hard labour, and general inhumane treatment of the enslaved. There were no exemptions from such manner of life with regard to age and gender. Put differently, the enslavement of Africans and their descendants was inclusive and non-discriminatory. Knibb describes this treatment succinctly. 'I have seen the old man seventy flogged; and infant of five years flogged, the slender youth; and he in his pride of [*adulthood*] manhood, the young woman just budding into life; and she who had reared a large family – nay, I have seen her who was with child flogged'[32] Regarding the inhumane treatment of children, Knibb writes:

The children are made to work at the early age of five; they are either sent to gather sour oranges for the hogs, or hoes put into their hands, and they assist in clearing and weeding the canes, or putting the overseer's garden in order.[33]

Knibb gives a very graphic account of this treatment especially in regard to women under the brutal hands of their male enslavers.

I have seen the drivers striking with bamboos on the nose and neck and even on the breasts of female [en] slaves. This act was a matter of conscience. It is a tremendous length and the driver makes it whirl around his head; every crack went straight to my heart.[34]

It was, therefore, surprising to Knibb that there was no immediate response of defence from the enslaved males who witnessed such inhumane treatment of their mothers and sisters. He says:

I was actually astonished and alarmed when I first saw its infliction, how a single white could actually use such power in the teeth of hundreds of slaves. After the flesh is so cut and torn, rum and salt pickle are rubbed upon the wounds.[35]

Believing that slavery is a sin, Knibb had no option but to defend the right of the enslaved for freedom. It was the right thing to do. He knew that oppression, evil is not permanent, does not have the final answer on human destiny, by affirming the biblical assertion; 'Let Justice prevail.'[36] This is a clear indication that the oppressor has been defeated and ultimately, liberation will triumph regardless of how long it takes. So for Knibb, anything less than immediate and total liberation and slavery itself is a sin. Coming to terms with this perspective of slavery, Knibb acknowledges: 'I say that slavery is a sin – a foul blot upon our nature. It is a sin that hangs heavily upon our natural character.'[37]

Here Knibb is dealing with the tragic dimension of the sin of slavery. It distorts, perverts and violates the dignity of the human beings. The only way to deal with this sinful act is through acceptance of God's liberation which the Sam Sharpe Revolt symbolizes. It is in this sense Sharpe's conscience played a pivotal role, as the barometer of right and wrong. As such, the Revolt, as it sought to transform a wicked and oppressive system on the principle of Divine righteousness, is a theological act.

Hope

In addition to freedom and righteousness, the Sam Sharpe Revolt theologically understood means hope. In an important essay on hope, Neville Callam posits the view that Sam Sharpe 'stands as a paradigm of hope.'[38] Callam premised this argument of Sharpe on the notions of captivity and promise which he defends by examining two dimensions of hope – the historical and the eschatological.[39] The historical dimension refers to Sam Sharpe and the Revolt he led. Callam puts it this way. 'Each year, Sharpe is remembered as one of the heroes who served the cause of emancipation of African-Jamaicans, and paved the way for all people to understand the painful joy of entertaining real hope in the midst of life.'[40] According to this remark, the idea of hope in history is the conviction that evil will not and cannot triumph over good. This is where, using the Pauline metaphor, Callam contends that Sharpe was a captive to hope.

As a captive to hope, Sharpe believed that his social conditions did not define his identity or determine his destiny. Callam points out that the enslaved nurtured this belief which was what empowered them to endure the inhumane existence of slavery. The enslaved understood the meaning of this hope which had implications for their immediate life and conditions. In fact, hope has revolutionary implications. It implies that liberation takes place in the here and now or during this present time and the gospel applies to life and the social and political conditions and system. Callam puts it succinctly; 'To ignore this perspective is to imprison hope, to make its realization captive to a future age.'[41]

Callam's remark acknowledges the relevance of hope to human affairs, which suggests that hope is not other-worldly. If so, this perspective would distort the meaning of hope in that the oppressed would understand hope as a future reality and has few implications for the present life. In case of the Sam Sharpe Revolt, this was not a future event but the realization of hope or more precisely, an approximation of hope in history because Christian hope is not fully realized in history (Rom. 8:24–25). Affirming this claim, Callam states:

> *The millions of involuntary exiles who were savagely torn from the ancestral civilization of West Africa and enslaved in the Caribbean [Americas] should not merely have dreamed of a*

distant future in which the hope of life in freedom would find fulfillment.[42]

This hope liberated and empowered the oppressed to fight for liberation. As Sam Sharpe is reported to have said; 'God never intended us to be slaves; that we had one master, Jesus Christ, to obey, and that we could not serve Christ and our master at the same time.'[43] Thus, hope in history can be understood to mean the realization that evil does not have the final, definitive nor ultimate word on human life and destiny.

The second dimension of hope is the eschatological. If, as Callam argues, Sharpe is a paradigm of hope, he embodied both the historical dimension as captive and the eschatological dimension by living what hope promised. In this sense, the Sam Sharpe Revolt not only means a realization of hope in history but living in anticipation of the hope to come. This dimension of hope is the promise where the enslaved and oppressed humanity affirm the Sovereignty of God, the Lordship of Jesus Christ and the beginning of the kingdom of God in history.[44] Actions like these have consequences. To hope, therefore, involves taking risks which may involve paying the ultimate price as with Sam Sharpe and those who dared to hope with him.[45] Here, the eschatological dimension of hope is an act of defiance of an evil system, the transformation of human society and exercise of faith in the liberating power of God.

Since paying the ultimate price is an inherent cost of what it means to hope, it is then, not enough to believe in hope. Rather, one must be prepared to pay whatever price that is required to hope. And, this price is a necessary condition to hope for liberation. Callam demonstrates his commitment to such a view.

> *Truly to hope is to make oneself vulnerable. Those who cherish real Christian hope refuse to allow negative experiences to destroy their hope, for it is stronger than fear, pain and despair...Because hope is alive in them, they can dare to take risky actions which seek the radical transformation of their unjust situation. In this process, they may lose their lives; but they are pursuing the commitment to a Lord whose justice guarantees the betterment of the oppressed, and not the mere preservation of their own physical existence.*[46]

How then should we understand the Sam Sharpe Revolt as a paradigm of hope? It can be understood as identifying with Christ through his death and resurrection. In this case, the Revolt is a sacramental witness of the death and resurrection of Jesus Christ. As Callam recognizes; 'Because of their unshakable confidence in the goodness and justice of God, they show forth a fortitude which reflects a clear understanding of the relation between crucifixion and resurrection in history.'[47] This remark acknowledges the Christological character of the Sam Sharpe Revolt as it comes to mean an expression of hope in history and the promise of hope to come.

Hope, therefore, is living in anticipation of the life promised by Jesus and secured through his life, death and resurrection. This means that hope is inclusive and holistic. It should not be limited to personal life or relegated to the future. If it were to be the former, then it would be utilitarian and if it were to be the latter, then it would be irrelevant. Christian hope concerns all aspects of life, shapes history and defines human destiny. In this sense, hope is both historical and eschatological.

Now, although the conditions of the enslaved may remain unchanged, and their pursuit of freedom failed,[48] as some have argued in the case of the Sam Sharpe Revolt, nevertheless, the Revolt defied the system of oppression and rejected its values to demonstrate that the enslaved refused to be dominated by or be subjected to any person other than God. This act of hope reflects the relationship between the enslaved and the powerful. The Revolt represented the power of the enslaved and the system of slavery represented the power of the oppressors.

Here, then, were two different powers contending for dominance. With the Sam Sharpe Revolt, it was the power of the enslaved subverting the dominant power structure as an expression of hope in history. Callam recognizes this power of the enslaved: 'True Christian hope rejects the ideology of power as either mere domination by, or meek submission to the might of the oppressor.'[49] Consequently, from the perspective of Black theology, this Revolt actually enacted God's will and demonstrated a radically profound challenge to a corrupt society and oppressive system as a revelation of not only hope but also of freedom.

Conclusion

This chapter constructs a theological meaning of the Sam Sharpe Revolt and affirms that the essential message of liberation resonated with the oppressed. Theologically understood, therefore, the Revolt was a revelation of God's active involvement in human affairs. Indeed, as an act of liberation, it demonstrated that God is radically and totally in solidarity with the oppressed, who heard the voice of God saying; 'I have indeed seen the misery of my people…I have heard them crying out… and I am concerned about their suffering. So, I have come down to liberate them…' (Exod. 3:7–8).

The prophet who wrote these words was engaged in this kind of encounter with God. In the face of suffering and oppression, this prophecy seeks to declare the loosening and weakening of the grip of the oppressor on the oppressed.

Similarly, the Sam Sharpe Revolt reveals God as using human agency to overthrow, dismantle, defeat and transform oppressive structures and systems (Jer. 1:9–10) and replacing them with freedom, justice, and hope (Rev. 21:1–5). Essentially, this Revolt has served to transform society and to give an understanding of the meaning of the human struggle for liberation as freedom, righteousness and hope.

Notes

1. Verene A. Shepherd and Ahmed Reid, 'Rebel Voices: Testimonies from the 1831–32 Emancipation War in Jamaica,' *Jamaica Journal*, 27, no. 2–3 (2004): 54–63.
2. H. M. Waddell, *Twenty-Nine Years in the West Indies and Central Africa* (London: Nelson and Co., 1863), 59.
3. Kortright Davis, *Emancipation Still Comin': Explorations in Caribbean Emancipatory Theology* (New York: Orbis Books, 1990), 9–10.
4. Davis, 8.
5. Ibid.
6. Ibid.
7. Noel Erskine, *Decolonizing Theology: A Caribbean Perspective* (New York: Orbis Books, 1981), 121.
8. Richard Hart, *Slaves Who Abolished Slavery: Blacks in Rebellion* (Kingston: University of the West Indies Press, 2002), 249.
9. Erskine, 121.

10. Ibid.
11. Ibid.
12. James Cone, *Black Theology & Black Power* 20th Anniversary Edition (San Francisco: Harper & Row, Publishers, 1989), 44.
13. Cone, 43–47. See also Dwight Hopkins, *Down, up and Over; Slave Religion and Black theology* (Minneapolis: Fortress Press, 2000), 174–77.
14. Henry Bleby, *Death Struggles of Slavery* (London: Hamilton, Adams and Co., 1853), 116–17.
15. S. Reid, 'Sam Sharpe – The Relevance of Conscience,' Montego Bay Rotary Club, St James, 16 December 1975.
16. Reid, 'Relevance of Conscience,' 6.
17. Ibid.
18. Reid, 'Relevance of Conscience,' 5.
19. Reid, 4.
20. T. Oxford, Defence *of the Baptist from the Charge of Inciting the Late Rebellion in a Discussion between the Rev. William Knibb and Mr P. Borthwic* (London: The Tourist Office, 1832).
21. Oxford, 4.
22. Knibb, 4. Here Knibb cites the words of Sharpe. Bleby, however, expresses the same idea but does not provide the direct words of Sharpe (Bleby, 117–18). While the exact words of Sharpe are uncertain, both accounts are concurrent with the idea expressed.
23. Cited on monument of the Kensington Historical Site (Jamaica: Tourism Product Development Company).
24. John Howard Hinton, *Memoir of William Knibb, Missionary in Jamaica (1849)* (London: Houlston and Stoneman, 18), 111–23.
25. Bleby, 7.
26. Hope Waddell, *Twenty-Nine Years in the West Indies and Central Africa* (London: T. Nelson & Co., 1863), 55–56.
27. Waddell, 51–52.
28. Bleby, 116. Bleby holds the opinion that Sharpe knew that the English king did not grant any freedom or that the slavers were holding freedom from the enslaved. For this reason, Bleby argues that Sharpe deceived himself. But this could not be the case given Sharpe's faith in Jesus Christ and his willingness to pay the ultimate price for freedom. Even if Sharpe's so-called master treated him well, it does not negate the authenticity of his faith and sincerity of his motive. What Bleby did not know is that Sharpe was not seeking freedom for and neither was he content with personal freedom when his people were in oppression. In fact, this manner of commitment is what distinguished Sharpe from others including people like Bleby.

29. Bleby, 112.
30. Oxford, 4.
31. Oxford, 20.
32. Oxford, 17.
33. Ibid.
34. Ibid.
35. Oxford, 16.
36. Oxford, 14.
37. Ibid.
38. Neville Callam, 'Hope: A Caribbean Perspective,' *Ecumenical Review* 50 (1998): 137,142.
39. Callam, 139.
40. Ibid.
41. Callam, 140.
42. Ibid.
43. Colonel Gardener, cited in Verene Shepherd and Ahmed Reid, 'Rebel Voices: Testimonies From the 1831–32 Emancipation War in Jamaica,' *Jamaica Journal, 27,* no. 2–3 (2004): 54–63.
44. Callam, 139–40
45. Shepherd and Reid, 56–58. Sharpe and his colleagues were prepared to pay whatever the price to obtain their freedom.
46. Callam, 140.
47. Callam, 140–41.
48. Mary Turner, *Slaves and Missionaries: The Disintegration of Jamaica Slave Society, 1787–1834* (Kingston: The Univeristy of the West Indies Press, 1998), 148.
49. Callam, 141.

Conclusion

In this book, the centrality of the Christian Faith in the Black struggle for liberation as symbolized by the Sam Sharpe Revolt was emphasized. The social context in which Sam Sharpe lived was considered and used to demonstrate the relationship between social context and faith. Sharpe could be likened to a 'Moses-like' figure who grew up in the household of Pharaoh the oppressors, and rebelled and revolted against this same system and society that contributed to making him into a liberator. In this sense, while Sharpe was living in a slave-holding society, he was not of it. Yet, the socio-political context, culture of resistance and religion of liberation which defined his 'world' played a central role in shaping and defining his identity and role in society.

The Sam Sharpe Revolt was grounded in faith as it is understood, developed and practised within the Black Faith Tradition of the Christian religion. It encompasses the beliefs and the theological meaning of this struggle for liberation. What is important is the consideration of faith not as a doctrinal belief but from an existential contextual perspective consisting of equality, justice and freedom that are born out of the Black experience. In this regard, the issues of liberation without faith have been explored as well as liberation with faith to demonstrate the Christocentric basis of the struggle for liberation.

This Christocentric understanding of faith as it applied to the Sam Sharpe Revolt confronted the reality of injustice which resulted in unnecessary death, indescribable suffering and unconscionable oppression of millions of people – God's sacred creation. As such, Sharpe not only applied his faith to the social reality of his time but he embodied it as indicated in the manner of his death, giving his life for the cause of liberation. Writing of Sharpe in this regard, Henry Bleby gave the following account: 'It was probable that a few would have to be punished, and perhaps put to death; and he or one was prepared to die rather than continue in slavery.'[1]

How does the Sam Sharpe Revolt relate to the Black Diaspora? It serves as a paradigm of kinship based on the common experience of oppression and struggle for liberation through faith in Jesus Christ. Here, an alternative understanding of Black identity and kinship emerged. Certainly, Blackness includes, but is not limited to colour or pigmentation. What is revealing is that Blackness in the Black theology advanced means commitment to the struggle for liberation and concurring with the understanding that God is Black as God entered into solidarity with oppressed people.

Additionally, faith in this God is a powerful weapon, a source of strength to resist and overcome oppression and also a powerful witness to the truth of the Christian Faith as revealed through Jesus Christ. The Sharpe Revolt bears witness to the central message of the 'good news' that the social structure and the holders of power are not God or representatives of God. While it can be argued that human power comes from God, the claim can equally be made that God's power transcends all powers especially that of the oppressors. For this reason, the gospel is the good news of God liberating the poor, that is, those who are regarded as non-persons, the immigrant, the uninsured, the beggars, the homeless, the exploited and dehumanized. The gospel tells them, encourages them to put their trust in God and to not worry over the cares of life. While their condition may remain unchanged, they are not defined by them because the gospel gives them a new sense of dignity, self-worth, and power to resist oppression. This dignity includes the news of God's victory over sin and over principalities and powers.

Ultimately, what does the Sam Sharpe Revolt have to do with faith in God, or more precisely, with theology, especially Black theology? While it has been easy, as it has been, to leave the interpretation of this event to non-religious scholars, it is compelling, even long overdue for theologians to engage with the interpretation of this event. Thus, theologically understood, the Sam Sharpe Revolt means freedom, righteousness and hope.

The challenge, however, is going beyond the discussion of this book which signifies a beginning attempt of a Black Atlantic theology. Put in another way, what conclusions can be drawn from this discussion? This leads us to ask questions such as what the Revolt teaches about God, ourselves, the meaning of our life, lessons learned and legacy bequeathed to future generations. This inquiry then, is a matter of faith asking questions about God, humanity and society. One of the truths that the Sam Sharpe Revolt teaches about God is that God is faithful to humanity, especially the poor, oppressed and marginalized as theologians such as Noel Erskine, Kelly Brown Douglas and others have pointed out. God cares and is committed to the world. It echoes the Johannine teaching that God loves the world (John 3:16–17). Certainly, evil exists in the world but it does not negate God's love and commitment to the world. Also, the presence and reality of evil does not mean that God has abandoned the world and that evil has the final word on human life and destiny. From this Revolt, however, we perceive that the enslaved were empowered to act to liberate themselves because they believed that God loves, values and cherishes each human being. Above all, the Revolt reveals God's solidarity with the oppressed and affirms the value and dignity of human life. Thus, we can generalize this principle to our own experience of the world.

If God enters into the Black experience and works against all things that mitigate against justice – the principalities and powers to promote equality and the fullness of life, then God is not a philosophical abstraction or merely a theological concept but rather a God fully committed and actively involved in human life and history. Indeed, from the Sam Sharpe Revolt, we understand that the God of the oppressors is not the true God and therefore the oppressors were not truly people of God. Thus, if the Sharpe Revolt gives any indication of the direction in which Black theology can move forward, this process begins with the recognition that the future of the Black Diaspora is inseparably connected to any understanding of God.

Along with what the Revolt teaches about God, it teaches other lessons about humanity in terms of our responsibilities to each other. Surely, the Sam Sharpe Revolt teaches that those with resources who are in a position of power and influence have a responsibility towards the less fortunate and most deprived among us. Sharpe, for example, could remain comfortable and content living as a 'house slave'. Instead, he accepted the responsibility and undertook the task of leading his people out of oppression. His actions echoed that of the biblical leader, Moses: 'He chose to be mistreated along with the people of God rather than to enjoy the pleasures of sin for a short time' (Heb. 12:25).

In fact, the wisdom writer challenged those in positions of power and authority to 'Speak up for those who cannot speak for themselves, for the rights of all who are destitute. Speak up and judge fairly; defend the rights of the poor and needy' (Prov. 31:8–9). This challenge is what the gospel tradition advances in the declaration; 'From everyone who has been given much, much will be demanded; and from the one who has been entrusted with much, much more will be asked' (Luke 12:48). In concurrence with this claim, the epistolary tradition gives the admonition to remember the poor (Gal. 2:10; 1 Tim. 6:17–18).[2]

This lesson of the responsibility of the more powerful to the less privileged needs to be learned in order to help the Black Diaspora to be conscious and committed to the most vulnerable ones among us. Learning this lesson reveals and deplores any misuse of religion to maintain and support oppressive systems and structures. Also, this lesson will facilitate continuing on the path of liberation and transformation of lives and society in making real the purpose of Jesus who offered the fullness of life to all persons (John 10:10).

While Sam Sharpe left no ideology, theology, philosophy, religious institution, party, or followers, he left a legacy to future generations. This legacy is the challenge to continue the work of equality, freedom and justice in the cause of liberation. Also, this is the liberation of people's minds so that they can have a clearer sense of identity and greater awareness of self-determination and freedom in how they live their lives. Sam Sharpe and the Revolt that he led are constant reminders that while the practice of slavery is legally abolished, the ideology and system that instituted, maintained and advanced it is not ended.[3] For example, the arrest of African American Louis Gates, Jr, the Fletcher University Professor at Harvard University, in his own home by a white police officer, is more than telling of the ubiquity of white supremacy in contemporary society. Someone saw Gates entering his home and reported to the police that he was a burglar. The fact that the police officer believed Professor Gates was a burglar even after Professor Gates provided proof of his identity and the right to be in his home, reinforces the reality of the demon of racism manifesting its ugly and devious presence whenever the opportunity arises.[4] In a report about this incident, the *Associated Press* asked a revealing question: 'If this man can be taken away by police from the porch of his own home, what does it say about the treatment that the average blacks can expect in 2009?'[5]

For this reason, theology in general and Black theology in particular must be constantly engaged in prophetic critique focusing on dismantling and eliminating beliefs and practices that represent acceptability and continuity of injustices and oppression. This critique is not only about race, class and gender. It must include religious, cultural and political imperialism as reflected in the contemporary manifestation of empire and materialistic and consumeristic Christianity.[6]

A challenge facing Black theology today is the social and political structure and ideology of empire represented by the United States and the system of global capitalism. Unfortunately, Black theology in Great Britain, the United States and the Caribbean is yet to address it as a theological issue.[7] Indeed, the context of these forms of Black theology is different due to the various social, political, cultural and religious contexts. Still, it is important to move from critique to offering an alternative vision of society that embraces the Black Diaspora and takes into account the impact various governments' public policies have on the world's poor and oppressed.

In this regard, if Black theology fails to advance this vision, then it runs the risk of being provincial and insular. But there is reason to hope. The legacy of the Sam Sharpe Revolt reminds us that it is not enough to critique but to move from critique to construction. Essentially, it is the alternative vision of reality that ensures a Black theology that is relevant to the Black Diaspora and serves God's liberating purpose as revealed in Jesus Christ.

So in light of the struggle for liberation, it must be clear, however, that while we seek to establish and live in a society where there is equality, freedom and justice, these will not be fully realized in history. Human frailty makes it impossible to achieve any ideal in history. This impossibility, however, does not mean we should resign ourselves to oppressive conditions for any reason. If we were not to hope, then it would mean not striving to achieve, not even partially, the fullness of life in history.

In this sense, theologically understood, Sam Sharpe Revolt is a glimpse of the promise of the fullness of life which gives meaning to earthly existence and underpins the struggle for liberation – freedom, righteousness and hope.

Notes

1. Sam Sharpe cited in Henry Bleby, *Death Struggles of Slavery* (London: Hamilton, Adams and Company, 1853), 113.
2. Pedrito U. Maynard-Reid, *Poverty and Wealth in James* (New York: Orbis Books, 1987); For a white Protestant perspective of this subject, see Joerg Rieger, *Remember The Poor: The Challenge to Theology in the Twenty-First Century* (Pennsylvania: Trinity Press International, 1988).
3. Anthony G. Reddie, *Black Theology, Slavery and Contemporary Christianity* (London: Ashgate, 2010).
4. Abbey Goodnough, 'Harvard Professor Jailed; Officer Is Accused of Bias,' *New York Times*, 21 July 2009.
5. 'Analysis: Gates Arrest a Signpost on Racial Road,' *Associated Press*, 22 July 2009.
6. Stephanie Y. Mitchem, *Name It and Claim It?: Prosperity Preaching in the Black* Church (Ohio: The Pilgrim Press, 2007).
7. While I know that no single work can address all issues, it concerns me that Caribbean theology has not even attempted to call attention to global issues such as empire and capitalism. See for example, Devon Dick, *The Cross and the Machete: Native Baptists' Identity, Ministry and Legacy* (Kingston: Ian Randle Publishers, 2010).

Select Bibliography

Afroz, Sultana. 'The Jihad of 1831–1832: The Misunderstood Baptists Rebellion in Jamaica.' *Journal of Moslem Minority Affairs 21, No. 2.* 2001.

Aldred, J. D. *Respect: Understanding Caribbean British Christianity.* Peterborough: Epworth, 2005.

Anderson, Victor. *Beyond Ontological Blackness: An Essay on African American Religious and Cultural Criticism*. New York: Contium,1995.

Andolsen, Barbara Hilkert. 'Social Justice, the Common Good and New Signs of Racism.' In *Interpreting White Privilege*. Edited by Laurie M. Cassidy and Alex Mikulich. New York: Orbis Books, 2007.

Aulen, Gustaf. Christus *Victor: An Historical Study of the Three Main Types of Idea of the Atonement.* Translated by A. G. Herbert. New York: Macmillan, 1969.

Austin-Broos, Diane J. *Jamaica Genesis: Religion and the Politics of Moral Order*. Kingston: Ian Randle Publishers, 1997.

Bailey, Randall. 'The Biblical Basis for a Political Theology of Liberation.' In *Blow the Trumpet in Zion: Global Vision and Action for the 21st-Century Black Church*. Edited by Iva E. Carruthers, Frederick D. Haynes and Jeremiah A. Wright. Minneapolis: Fortress Press, 2005.

Beckford, Robert. *Jesus Is Dread: Black Theology and Black Culture in Britain.* London: *DLT,* 1998.

———. *Dread and Pentecostal: A Political Theology for the Black Church in Britain*. London: SPCK, 2000.

Beckles, Hilary McD. 'Caribbean Anti-Slavery: The Self-Liberation Ethos of Enslaved Blacks.' In *Caribbean Slavery in the Atlantic Worlds*. Edited by Verene Shepherd and Hilary McD. Beckles. Kingston: Ian Randle Publishers, 2000.

Beckles, Hilary McD. and Verene A. Shepherd. *Saving Souls: The Struggle to End the Transatlantic Trade in Africans*. Kingston: Ian Randle Publishers, 2007.

Benn, Denis. *The Caribbean: An Intellectual History, 1774–2003.* Kingston: Ian Randle Publishers, 2004.

Besson, Jean. *Martha Brae's Two Histories: European Expansion and*

Caribbean Culture – Building in Jamaica. Chapel Hill: University of North Carolina Press, 2002; Kingston: Ian Randle Publishers, 2003.

Bisnauth, Dale. *History of Religions in the Caribbean.* Kingston: LMH Publishing Limited, 1989.

———. 'The 1831–32 Jamaica Slave Revolt: The Case For A Holy War.' *Caribbean Journal of Religious Studies,* 21:1 (October, 2007).

Bleby, Henry. *Death Struggles of Slavery.* London: Hamilton, Adams & Co., 1853.

———. *Scenes in the Caribbean Sea: Being Sketches from a Missionary's Notebook*. London: Hamilton, Adams and Company, 1854.

Bolt, Cawley St Clair. *Some Missing Understanding of Negro Characteristic in Jamaica, 1834–1870 with Particular Reference to Selected Baptist Missions.* PhD thesis, Oxford Centre for Christian Missions, University of Wales, 2006.

Braithwaite, Edward. 'Sam Sharpe.' Kingston: Jamaica Broadcasting Corporation, 1973.

———. *Nanny, Sam Sharpe and the Struggle for People's Liberation.* Kingston: Agency for Public Information, 1976.

———. *Wars of Respect: Nanny and Sharpe*. Kingston: Agency for Public Information, 1977.

———. 'The Anatomy of the Slave Revolt.' *Jamaica Historical Society Bulletin 8*. December, 1981.

———. 'The Slave Rebellion in the Great River Valley of St James – 1831–32.' *Jamaica Historical Review,* Vol. XII, 1982.

Briggs, John H. Y. 'Baptist and the Campaign to abolish the Slave Trade.' *Baptist Quarterly* Vol. 42, October (2007).

British Parliamentary Papers. Nos. 285 & 561. Vol. XLVII, 1831–32.

Brown Douglas, Kelly. 'To Reflect the Image of God.' In *Living the Intersection: Womanism and Afrocentrism in Theology. Edited by* Cheryl Sander. Minneapolis: Fortress Press, 1995.

———. *What's Faith Got To Do With It? Black Bodies/Christian Souls.* New York: Orbis Books, 2005.

Brueggemann, Walter. *The Prophetic Imagination*. Philadelphia: Fortress Press, 1978.

Burchell, William F. *Memoir of Thomas Burchell: Twenty-Two Years a Missionary in Jamaica*. London: Benjamin L. Green, 1849.

Burton, Richard D. E. *Afro-Creole: Power, Opposition and Play in the Caribbean.* Ithaca: Cornell University Press, 1997.

Bush, Barbara. *Slave Women in Caribbean Society 1650–1838.* Bloomington: Indiana University Press, 1990.

Callahan, Allen D. *The Talking Book: African American and the Bible.* New Haven: Yale University Press, 2006.

Callam, Neville. 'Hope: A Caribbean Perspective.' *Ecumenical Review* 50, 1998.

Campbell, Mavis C. *The Maroons of Jamaica: A History of Resistance & Betrayal.* New Jersey: Africa World Press Inc., 1990.

Cassidy, Laurie M. and Alex Mikulich, eds. *Interpreting Whiteness: Catholic Theologians Break the Silence.* New York: Orbis Books, 2007.

Clarke, John. *Memorials of Baptist Missionaries in Jamaica, Including the Sketch of Labours of the Early Religious.* London: Yates and Alexander, 1869.

Cone, James H. *Black Theology & Black Power.* New York: Harper & Row, 1969.

———. *Liberation: A Black Theology of Liberation.* New York: J.B. Lippincott Co., 1970.

———. *God of the Oppressed.* New York: Seabury Press, 1975.

———. *Martin, Malcolm & America. New York: Orbis Books, 1981.*

———. *For My People: Black Theology and the Black Church – Where Have We Been and Where Are We Going?* New York: Orbis Books, 1984.

———.'Theology as the Expression of God's Liberating Activity for the Poor.' In *The Vocation of the Theologian.* Edited by Theodore W. Jennings, Jr. Philadelphia: Fortress Press, 1985.

Craton, Michael. *Testing the Chains.* Ithaca: Cornell University Press, 1982.

Davis, Kortright. *Emancipation Still Comin': Exploration in Caribbean Emancipatory Theology.* New York: Orbis Books, 1991.

Dick, Devon Merrick. *The Cross and the Machete: Native Baptists' Identity, Ministry and Legacy.* Kingston: Ian Randle Publishers, 2010.

Edwards, Bryan. *The History, Civil and Commercial of the West Indies* (1819, Vol. 2). New York: AMS Press, 1966.

Ellington, Mark. *The Riches of Augustine: His Contextual & Pastoral Theology.* Kentucky: Westminster John Knox Press, 2005.

Erskine, Noel Leo. *Decolonizing Theology: A Caribbean Perspective.* New York: Orbis Books, 1981.

———. *From Garvey to Marley: Rastafari Theology.* Florida: University of Florida Press, 2005.

———. *Black Theology and Pedagogy.* New York: Palgrave Macmillan, 2008.

Evans, James H. Jr. *We Have Been Believers.* Minneapolis: Fortress Press, 1992.

Fanon, Frantz. *Black Skin White Mask.* New York: Grove Press, 1967.

Furley Oliver W. 'Moravian Missionaries and Slaves in the West Indies.' *Caribbean Studies* No. 5:2, July, 1965.

Gayle, Clement. *George Liele: Pioneer Missionary to Jamaica.* Kingston: Jamaica Baptist Union, 1982.

Garvey, Marcus. *Philosophy & Opinion of Marcus Garvey, Vol. 11*, ed. Amy Jacques Garvey. New York: Antheneum, 1980.

Gilbourne, Philip. 'Two faces of Sam Sharpe.' *Sunday Gleaner, 13 August 1982.*

Gilroy, Paul. *The Black Atlantic: Modernity and Double Consciousness.* New York: Verso, 1993.

Gonzalez, Justo L. *The Story of Christianity: The Early Church to the Dawn of the Reformation*, Vol. 1. Massachusetts: Price Press, 1984.

Goodnough, *Abbey.* 'Harvard Professor Jailed; Officer is Accused of Bias.' *New York Times,* 21 July 2009.

Gordon, Shirley. *Our Cause for His Glory: Christianisation and Emancipation in Jamaica.* Kingston: University of the West Indies Press, 1998.

———. *God Almighty Made Me Free: Christianity in Pre-emancipation Jamaica.* Indianapolis: Indiana University Press, 1996.

Hart, Richard. *Slaves Who Abolished the Slavery: Blacks in Rebellion.* Kingston: University of the West Indies Press, 2002.

Higman, B. W. *Montpelier Jamaica: A Plantation Community in Slavery and Freedom 1739–1912.* Kingston: The Press, 1998.

———. *Plantation Jamaica 1750–1850: Capital and Control in a Colonial Economy.* Kingston: University of the West Indies Press, 2005.

Hill, Frank. 'Sam Sharpe led first strike in Jamaica for wages.' *Sunday Gleaner*, 26 October, 1975.

Hinton, John Howard. *Memoir of William Knibb, Missionary in Jamaica (1849)*. Bristol: Houlston and Stoneman, 1849.

Hopkins, Dwight N. *Down, Up, and Over: Slave Religion and Black Theology*. Minneapolis: Fortress Press, 2000.

———. *Head and Heart: Black Theology – Past, Present and Future*. New York: Palgrave Macmillan, 2002.

James, C.L.R. 'The Atlantic Slave Trade.' In *The Future Present*. London: Allison & Busby, 1977, 243.

———. 'The Making of the Caribbean People.' In *Spheres of Existence*. London: Allison & Busby, 1980, 174.

———. *The Black Jacobs: Toussaint L'Ouverture and the San Domingo Revolution*. New York: Vintage Books, 1983.

James, Leslie. 'Text and the Resistance of Change: Bible and Decolonization in Post-World War II Caribbean Discourse.' In *Religion, Culture and Tradition.* Edited by Hemshand Gossai and Samuel Nathaniel Murrell. London: MacMillan Press Ltd., 2000, 143–66

Kennedy, Fred. *Daddy Sharpe: A Narrative of the Life and Adventures of Samuel Sharpe, A West Indian Slave Narrative Written by Himself, 1832.* Kingston: Ian Randle Publishers, 2008.

Kirton, Allan. 'Current Trends in Caribbean Theology and the Role of the Church.' *Caribbean Quarterly* 37, No. 1. March 1991.

Lawes, Marvia. 'An Historical Evaluation of Jamaica Baptists: A Spirituality of Resistance.' *Black Theology: An International Journal*. London: Equinox Publishing Ltd., 2008.

Lawson, Winston A. *Religion and Race: African and European Roots in Conflict – A Jamaican Testament*. New York: Peter Lang Publishing, 1996.

Levy, Andrea. *The Long Song*. New York: Farrar, Straus and Giroux, 2010.

Lewis, Gordon K. *Main Currents in Caribbean Thought: The Historical Evolution of Caribbean Society in its Ideological Aspects, 1492–1999*. Baltimore: Johns Hopkins University Press, 1983.

Lewis, Rupert. M*arcus Garvey.* New Jersey: Africa World Press, Inc., 1988.

Liele, George. 'Letter from George Liele to Dr John Rippon.' *Baptist Register*, 18 December 1791.

Lincoln, C. Eric and Mamiya, Lawrence H. *The Black Church in the African American Experience.* Durham: Duke University Press, 1990.

Mair, Lucille Mathurin. *The Rebel Woman in the British West Indies during Slavery.* Kingston: Institute of Jamaica for the African-Caribbean Institute of Jamaica, 1975.

Manley, Michael. 'Nanny, Sam Sharpe helped set road to freedom.' *The Jamaican Gleaner*, 19 October 1975.

Marley, Robert Nesta. *Small Axe.* Bob Marley and the Wailers, Prod. Direct Source Special Production Inc.

———. Robert N. Marley. '*Redemption Song.*' Bob Marley and the Wailers, Prod. Islands Record Inc., 1980.

Maynard-Reid, Pedrito U. *Poverty and Wealth in James.* New York: Orbis Books, 1987.

McClendon, James Wm., Jr. *Biography as Theology*. Philadelphia: Trinity International Press, 1990.

Mitchem, Stephanie, Y. *Name It and Claim It? Prosperity Preaching in the Black Church.* Ohio: Pilgrim Press, 2007.

Nettleford, Rex. *Inward Stretch Outward Reach: A Voice From The Caribbean*. London: Macmillan Press, 1993.

Oden, Thomas C. *How Africa Shaped the Christian Mind*. Illinois: IVP Books, 2007.

T. Oxford, *Defence of the Baptist Missionaries from the Charge of Inciting the Late Rebellion in Jamaica.* London: The Tourist Office, 1832.

Paris, Peter. *The Spirituality of African Peoples: The Search For A Common Moral Discourse.* Minneapolis: Fortress Press, 1995.

Patterson, Orlando. *Social of Slavery: An Analysis of the Origins, Development, and Structure of Negro Slave Society in Jamaica.* London: Macgibbon & Kee, 1973.

Payne, Ernest. *Freedom in Jamaica: Some Chapters in the Story of Baptist Missionary Society.* London: Carey Press, 1946.

Pinn, Anthony. *Varieties of African American Religious Experience.* Minneapolis: Fortress Press, 1998.

Potter, Philip and Barbara Wartenberg-Potter. *Freedom is for Freeing.* New York: The United Methodist Church, 1990.

Prescod, Patrick. 'The Right Hand of God.' In *Lift Every Voice and Sing II: An African American Hymnal*. New York: The Church Pension

Fund, 1993, 61.
Raboteau, Albert J. *Slave Religion: The 'Invisible Institution' in the Antebellum South*. New York: Oxford University Press.
Reckford, Mary. 'The Jamaica Slave Rebellion of 1831.' *Past & Present*, 40. July, 1968.
Reddie, Anthony G. *Growing into Hope: Liberation and Change.* Peterborough: Methodist Publishing House, 1998.
———. *Black Theology in Transatlantic Dialogue.* New York: Palgrave Macmillan, 2006.
———. *Working Against the Grain: Re-imaging Black Theology in the 21st Century*. London: Equinox Publishing Ltd., 2008.
———. *Black Theology Slavery and Contemporary Christianity.* London: Ashgate, 2010.
Reddie, Richard S. *Abolition: The Struggle to Abolish Slavery in the British Colonies*. Oxford: Lion Hudson plc, 2007.
Reid, C. S. '*Sam Sharpe* – The Relevance of Conscience,' Montego Bay Rotary Club, St James, 16 December 1975.
———. 'Sam Sharpe Lauded as Jamaica's First True Labor Leader...' *Star Western Bureau*, 24 May 1982.
———. *Samuel Sharpe: From Slave to National Hero.* Kingston: The Bustamante Institute of Public and International Affairs, 1988.
Reid, V.S. *Peter of Ephraim*. Kingston: Jamaica Publishing House, 1971.
Reid-Salmon, Delroy A. *Home Away from Home: The Caribbean Diasporan Church in the Black Atlantic Tradition*. London: Equinox Publishing Ltd., 2008.
Roberts, J. Deotis. 'A Black Ecclesiology of Involvement.' *Journal of Black Religious Thought* 32, Spring-Summer 1975.
———. *Afrocentric Christianity: A Theological Appraisal for Ministry.* Valley Forge: Judson Press, 2000.
Russell, Horace. 'Baptist and Liberation.' *Baptist Quarterly: Journal of the Baptist Historical Society*, XXX111, No. 7. July, 1990.
Sampson, Anthony. *Mandela: The Authorized Biography*. New York: Alfred A. Knopf, 1999.
Sanders, Cheryl. *Empowering Ethics for a Liberating People: A Path to African American Social Transformation.* Minneapolis: Fortress Press, 1995.
Schwarz, Bill, ed. *West Indian Intellectuals in Britain*. Manchester:

Manchester University Press, 2003.

Shannon, David T. and Gayraud S. Wilmore. *Black Witness to the Apostolic Faith.* Michigan: Eerdmans, 1985.

Senior, B.M. *Jamaica as it was, as it is, and as it may be.* London: T. Hurst, 1835.

Shepherd, Verene. *I want to Disturb My Neighbor: Lectures on Slavery, Emancipation and Postcolonial Jamaica.* Kingston: Ian Randle Publishers, 2007.

Shepherd, Verene A. and Ahmed Reid. 'Rebel Voices: Testimonies from the 1831–32 Emancipation War in Jamaica.' *Jamaica Journal,* 27, No. 2–3, 2004.

Sherlock, Phillip. *Shout for Freedom; A Tribute to Sam Sharpe.* London: Macmillan Education Ltd., 1976.

Sherlock, Phillip and Hazel Bennett. *The Story of the Jamaican People.* Kingston: Ian Randle Publishers, 1998.

Simmonds, Lorna Elaine. 'The Afro-Jamaican and the Internal Market System, Kingston 1780–1834.' In *Jamaica in Slavery and Freedom: History, Heritage and Culture.* Edited by Kathleen E. A. Monteith and Glen Richards. Kingston: University of the West Indies Press, 2002.

Stewart, Robert J. *Religion and Society in Post-Emancipation Jamaica.* Tennessee: University of Tennessee Press, 1992.

Stewart, Dianne M. *Three Eyes for the Journey: African Dimensions of the Jamaican Religious Experience.* New York: Oxford University Press, 2005.

Sugirtharajah, R.S., ed. *Marist Critical Tools: Are They Helpful in breaking the Stronghold of Idealist Hermeneutics.* New York: Orbis Books, 1995.

Taylor, Burchell. 'The Liberated Community as Subversive and Liberating in an Unjust Society.' In *Caribbean Theology: Preparing for the Challenges Ahead.* Edited by Howard Gregory Kingston: Canoe Press, 1995.

Torres-Saillant, Silvio. *An Intellectual History of the Caribbean.* New York: Palgrave Macmillan, 2006.

Thomas, *Oral 'Contextual Contestations in Biblical Hermeneutics within a Caribbean Context: A case for a Biblical Resistant Hermeneutic.'* PhD thesis, University of Birmingham, 2007.

Thompson, Alvin O. *Flight to Freedom: African Runaways and Maroons in the Americas*. Kingston: University of the West Indies Press, 2006.

Tucker, Robert C., ed. *The Marx-Engels Reader* 2nd ed. New York: Norton, 1978.

Turner, Mary. *Slaves and Missionaries: The Disintegration of Jamaican Slave Society, 1787–1834*. Kingston: University of the West Indies Press, 1998.

Tutu, Desmond. *God Has A Dream: A Vision of Hope for Our Time.* New York: Doubleday, 2004.

Volf, Miroslav. *Exclusion & Embrace: A Theological Exploration of Identity, Otherness and Reconciliation*. Nashville: Abingdon Press, 1996.

Waddell, Hope. *Twenty-Nine Years in the West Indies and Central Africa: A Review of Missionary Life and Adventure 1829–1858.* London: T. Nelson & Son, 1863.

Wallis, Jim. *God's Politics: Why the Right Gets It Wrong and the Left Does not Get It.* New York: Harper Collins Publishers, 2005.

Ware, Frederick L. *Methodologies of Black Theology*. Cleveland: The Pilgrim Press, 2002.

Waters, Kenneth L. *Afrocentric Sermons: The Beauty of Blackness in the Bible*. Valley Forge: Judson Press, 1993.

Weir, Emmette. 'Towards a Caribbean Liberation Theology.' *Caribbean Journal of Religious* Studies 12, No. 1. April, 1991.

West, Cornel. *Prophesy Deliverance: An Afro-American Revolutionary Christianity*. Philadelphia: Westminster Press, 1982.

Williams, Delores. 'Womanist Theology: Black Women's Voices.' In *Black Theology: A Documentary History, 1980–1992*. Edited by James Cone and Gayraud Wilmore. New York: Orbis Books, 1993.

Williams, Eric. *Capitalism and Slavery.* North Carolina: University of North Carolina Press, 1944; Kingston: Ian Randle Publishers, 2005.

Williams, Lewin. *Caribbean Theology.* New York: Peter Lang, 1994.

Wilmore, Gayraud. *Black Religion and Black Radicalism: An Interpretation of the Religious History of Afro-American people.* New York: Orbis Books, 1973.

Woolley, E. 'The Land of the Free.' Cincinnati: Caleb Clark, 1847.

Wright, Jeremiah. *Africans who shaped our Faith.* Illinois: Urban Ministries Inc., 1995.

Wright, M. *Becoming Black: Creating Identity in the African Diaspora.* North Carolina: Duke University Press, 2004.
Wright, Philip. *Knibb The 'Notorious' Slaves' Missionary, 1803–1845.* London: Sidgwick and Johnson, 1973.

OTHER REFERENCES

THESES

Cawley St Clair Bolt, *Some Missing Underst*anding of Negro *Characteristic in Jamaica, 1834–1870 with Particular Reference to Select Bap*tist *Missions*, PhD (University of Wales), 2006.
Oral Thomas, *Contextual Contestations in Biblical Hermeneutics within a Caribbean Context: A case for a Biblical Resistant Hermeneutic,* PhD (University of Birmingham), 2007.

JOURNALS

Baptist Register, 18 December 1791.
Baptist Quarterly: Journal of the Baptist Historical Society, XXX111, No. 7. July, 1990.
Baptist Quarterly Vol. 42, October, 2007.
Black Theology: An International Journal. London: Equinox Publishing Ltd., 2008.
Caribbean Quarterly 37, No. 1. March 1991.
Caribbean Journal of Religious Studies, 21:1. October, 2007.
Caribbean Studies, No. 5.2, July, 1965.
Ecumenical Review 50, 1998.
Jamaica Historical Review, Vol. XII, 1982.
Jamaica Historical Society Bulletin, 8 December 1981.
Jamaica Journal, 27. No. 2–3, 2004.
Journal of Black Religious Thought 32, Spring–Summer 1975.
Journal of Moslem Minority Affairs 21, No. 2. 2001.
Past & Present, 40. July, 1968.

NEWSPAPERS

Associated Press, 22 July 2009
Jamaica Currant, 6 January 1832.
Jamaica Watchman, 4 January 1832
Jamaica Watchman, 2 June 1832.

New York Times, 21 July 2009.
Star Western Bureau, 24 May 1982.
Sunday Gleaner, 19 October 1975.
Sunday Gleaner, 13 August 1982.
Sunday Gleaner, 26 October 1975.

GOVERNMENT DOCUMENTS

British Parliamentary Papers. Nos. 285 & 561. Vol. XLVII, 1831–32.

Index

Lightning Source UK Ltd.
Milton Keynes UK
UKOW051723090712

195689UK00001B/28/P

9 789766 375386